The Hills:
More Tales from the Blue Stacks

The Hills:
More Tales from the Blue Stacks

Stories of Ireland

ROBERT BERNEN

CHARLES SCRIBNER'S SONS   NEW YORK

Copyright © 1983 Robert Bernen
First United States edition published
by Charles Scribner's Sons 1983

Library of Congress Cataloging in Publication Data

Bernen, Robert.
  The hills.

    Contents: Fox — The scythe — Brock — [etc.]
    1. Blue Stack Mountains (Ireland) — Fiction.
I. Title.
PS3552.E7312H5   1983   813'.54   83-16424
ISBN 0-684-18005-7

1 3 5 7 9 11 13 15 17 19 F/C 20 18 16 14 12 10 8 6 4 2

Printed in the United States of America.

Contents

Foreword

The stories collected here were written on a hill farm nine miles north of Donegal Town, one of a loose string of isolated farms that skirt the range of hills known as the Blue Stacks. To their south the land slopes downwards across progressively more fertile and more densely populated land to the sea seven miles away. To their north are six miles of uninhabited hills on the far side of which live a broad area of Irish speaking farmers and tradesmen.

Though at first sight the hills appear to be the dividing line between Irish speakers to the north and English speakers to the south, further acquaintance reveals that the Irish speaking farmers have spilled over the hills, so that the southernmost limit of that Irish speaking area is marked by the highest line of farm houses on the south-facing slopes. For while hill and mountain ranges are often taken as convenient boundaries, even national ones, the animals that graze those ranges and the shepherds that follow them are not aware of such divisions. For them the real dividing line is found where the coarse heathers and stony ground of the upland give way to the kinder grass and arable land of lower altitudes. It is there that the shepherd stops and the farmer takes over.

The farm the author lived on was just inside the dividing line between the Irish and the English speakers, but that area was in a sense cut off from both groups, from the English speakers to the south by the simple difference of language, from the Irish speakers to the north by the obstacle of the roadless hills, an obstacle that became gradually more important as the use of cars for transport spread and people grew less and less used to walking long distances over difficult ground. Being out of touch with its parent area to the north, this little fringe of houses on the southern slope of the hills was also cut off from many of the modern innovations that time was bringing to that larger area. Schools, for instance, where the knowledge of the language was being kept alive while modern ideas and ways were being introduced at the same time to replace older ones. South of the hill barrier, by contrast, there were only English language schools, attended by the Irish speakers intermittently and with diffidence, if at all. For them, knowledge of their language was kept alive and transmitted as it had been for centuries, around the hearth, from parent to child. Along with the language went many old traditions and ways of thought, as well as ways of work, and generally ways of being, of life. It was the world in a simpler stage than usually known or experienced in our time.

In the early 1970s, when the author and his wife bought their farm and began farming, this simple way of life was largely as it always had been. The three-room houses, their low walls built without mortar from rough stone quarried on the site, were roofed with a thatch of rushes cut not far from the door. In them the only source of heat was the large kitchen hearth, where all the meals were prepared in heavy cast iron pots. All the work of the farm, milking, planting, mowing, reaping, was done by hand. Water for washing and cooking was carried in from spring wells. Speech and thought as well were still based on the traditions of life and like them were largely unin- fluenced by the changes taking place in the rest of the world. The virtual absence of radio and the infrequency of newspapers allowed old customs and beliefs to remain alive. The daily conversations of the farmers and their families were not drawn from world events but from their own lives farming sheep and cattle on the rough hill and cultivating small crops for home use on the limited arable land, or from the legends and orally transmitted experience of past generations.

The author came to see this little semi-isolated world of simple farming and sheep-herding life as the place where the road ends and the hill begins. There, in almost constant contact with his neighbours, gradually accommodating to their ways and abandoning his own as less appropriate to the life he was leading then, he was able to observe and experience the world as would not otherwise have been possible for him. Some of those observations and personal experiences are preserved in these stories.

The Hills:
More Tales from the Blue Stacks

FOX

Peadar Nohar More counted the lambs on his park. They were all wether-lambs – all the wethers on the farm – and they were all in about their sixth month. They had been born in April and May, and it was now early October. The autumn had been fine and dry, the hay had been carried in and built into stacks, the turf had been thatched and there had even been time to put a new coat of green rush thatch on the old cow byre. That done, Peadar had gathered his sheep into the crumbling, roofless walls of an old kitchen, all that remained of the long deserted house, and separated lambs from ewes, and then ewe-lambs from wether-lambs. The ewe-lambs he had driven down to their winter grazing on his sister's farm in the valley below, the wether-lambs had remained above on the hills with him. Only for a few days, however, only until the harvest fair, when he would drive them over the hills to the fair and sell them there.

The wethers had begun to fatten in the week or so they had been in the fenced-in park, as Peadar called his six acres of green meadow. Six acres of green meadow out of an area of almost a square mile of farm, all of it, except those six acres of green land, rough knolls of bog, outcroppings of grey lichen-covered rock, stretches of coarse, heavy red grass – the only grass that would grow in the acid bog of the high hill – and round, clear, unfathomably deep small lakes. The six green acres had been won from its original rough state, its cover of heather, by the hard work of the spade, and by the lime quarried and burnt high on the side of the hill, carried down in creels, spread by hand, as well as by the incessant dunging with the manure cleaned from the byre, and by the never missed annual mowing of the hay, a mowing carried out every year by Peadar himself with sharpened steel scythe, razor close to the smooth surface of the meadow, cleaning the ground as he mowed of any roughness, discouraging the growth of any

1

weed. This year, in the fine summer weather that had, as an exception to the rule of wet summers, persisted throughout the last three months, the hay had been mown in late July and early August and had been won and carried in and built into stacks soon after. The freshly mown meadow had quickly put up a fine, soft green aftergrass ideal for young lambs. Peadar smiled inwardly as he watched his wethers grazing that aftergrass now, with apparently incessant appetite. You could see them mending on it, as he put it to himself.

Slowly his eyes scanned the young sheep one by one, their small new horns and intensely black faces, assessing and counting all at once as he looked. The count mounted up by scores, two score, three score, and so on upwards to just over the five score mark, just over the hundred, of sheep. Peadar paused. He walked to a new stand-point twenty yards or so to his left and started his count again, again by scores, but more rapidly this time, his lips moving as he counted, his right arm rising involuntarily to the count, his fingers half pointing to individual lambs where their closeness to each other made counting difficult in the denseness of the white fleeces. Again the count mounted to just over a hundred lambs, and again he was not satisfied. He walked down to the wooden gate in the upper stretch of fence and went through it into the park itself. Slowly he walked through the lambs, counting again as he went. Finishing the count, he stopped to consider again. He had one hundred and three wether-lambs, he should have had one hundred and four. He reconsidered. He was sure he had the full count when he had taken the ewe-lambs out of the wethers a few days before.

His first throught was of the drains, the long, deep, open drains that ran across and down the land carrying off the excess moisture that flowed incessantly downward from the steep hill above. At once he walked the entire length of those drains, but found nothing. The wether had not fallen into the drain. His next thought was of a fault in the fence. The missing wether could have slipped away through a hole in the fence, or under it. But he himself had taken a day not long since, one of the few wet days that summer when nothing could be done with the hay, to walk the length of the fence with his spade, cutting sods from the rough heathery ground on the uphill side, carefully tucking them in under the lowest horizontal wire of the fence, between that wire and the ground, sealing it, as it were, closing every hole or space that had been opened up by the persistence of rabbits or badgers or foxes, holes just large enough for a young lamb to squeeze through and away. Easy enough slipping out, he reflected, but hard enough, for some reason, for them to find their way back again. Slip through and then, later, find themselves isolated from the rest of the sheep. Then, wanting desperately to rejoin the flock, they could never find their way back, find the place they had come through before. Only the old ewes could do that, the ones that had learned, but never the lambs. As he had cut the last of the sods with his long, slender spade and pushed it neatly into place beneath the fence he laughed softly to himself. 'The young sheep are kind of silly of themselves at times,' he thought. And then, looking at his day's work, 'Nothing will pass that,' he thought to himself. 'A dog itself wouldn't squeeze under that fence now.'

As he returned through the gate and up the slope towards his stone thatched house he inspected the bottom of the fence again, not walking it but merely running his eye the length of the wire. 'No,' he repeated again this morning, 'a dog wouldn't go under that. Whatever way that lamb got out!' The only thing to do was to go around the hill. Perhaps he had left the lamb on the hill without knowing it when he had gathered in the others. It was easy to miss one lamb. Or had his sister left the park gate open one morning when she went through on her way to the byre to carry hay to the cows and milk them, and the lamb slipped away then? No matter, he would find the wether-lamb. There was a long day ahead still.

As he reached the house he turned for a final look over the park and saw, some two hundred yards distant, his sister coming from the old newly-rethatched cow-byre, the milking bucket in her hand, slowly making her way across the meadow again and towards the house. The new thatch on the byre was a cause for satisfaction, a job well done, and done in good time, but the old byre beside the cow byre – what Peadar called the wee byre – was badly in need of new thatch. It had been several years since he had thatched it last. That was another job to be done this fall or winter.

Before going into the house he went to a low rounded craw built of rough grey stones and covered with a thick blanket of flat thatch, opened the small improvised wooden door, held closed throughout the night by a wooden prop firmly wedged against it. As he opened the door he said softly, 'Come on out now.' A brown collie dog – reddish-brown, but what Peadar referred to as his yellow dog – lifted his head, rose from his bed of hay-filled sack, stretched his forelegs straight out before him, sinking forwards, then his hindlegs straight out behind, yawning as he did so and emitting a little involuntary sound of swiftly escaping breath, a kind of small expression of greeting and good will and expectation all in one. Then he emerged, looking up at Peadar and letting his tail undulate gently from side to side.

'Come in the house, now,' Peadar talked to the dog, 'she'll be up now with the milk. We'll take our tea now. Come in now.' As the dog ran quickly around to the far side of the house, ignoring for the moment Peadar's injunction to follow him in, Peadar himself went through the low doorway. Putting his stick against a high wooden cupboard that stood along the wall flanking the door, he went to the hearth, where glowing orange coals of turf, carefully buried under their own ashes eight hours before, had been slumbering through the night, waiting to rekindle the new fire, the next in a long chain of daily fires, each one started from and continuing the one before, never extinguished even on the warmest of summer days.

Poking the iron tongs that had been standing, like a pair of long thin legs jointed to a tiny head, by the side of the hearth, into the ashes, he shook them away through the rungs of the iron grate down into the ash-pit below. Quickly, with deft movements of the tongs gathering the glowing coals that remained into a heap in the centre of the grate, he took fresh, dry chunks of turf from a creel in the corner of the room and built them into a kind of vertical chimney around the live coals. At once an upward flowing stream of fresh white smoke announced the flames that would soon appear. Taking a black aluminum tea-pot encrusted with layers of hard soot from the hob beside the grate, Peadar rinsed it out with water dipped from a bucket standing near the kitchen door and filled it with fresh water. He reached his thick large hand into a tin box and drew out a fistful of black tea. Dropping the tea into the aluminum pot, he replaced its lid and settled it above the newly made fire to come slowly to the boil, the smoke from the fire that was curving upward and around the pot made swifter in its ascent by the round obstacle itself.

Peadar's sister came in with the milk, the yellow dog following at her feet. As she set the pail down on the kitchen table and went to get the large porcelain pitcher she would pour the milk into she was saying something, about one of the cows, in a high voice which was yet partly a mutter, a mixture of talking to herself and yet announcing to the world at large – in this case Peadar alone. In her youth, decades before, she had gone out on the hill in search of the grey-black lichen that clung to the tops of the granite rocks and that, boiled for long hours over the turf fire, gave a deep red-brown colour to the wool she herself spun and knitted into socks and pullovers, and, on this particular expedition, had been overtaken by mist, a thick hill mist in the high hill plain where paths were few, and that made it hard or impossible for all but the most experienced of sheepfarmers to orient themselves in the few yards of ground that the mist left visible to them in any direction. Wandering uncertainly about, her sack of crottle, the black, red-staining lichen, on her shoulder, she had finally been overtaken by darkness, and then by a cold rain, and had spent the night sheltering from the weather under an overhanging bank of bog. A wind had come up, and she crouched as well into the sheltering bit of bog as she could, pulling her clothes around her against the seeping drops of water that fell from the overhanging turf. In the morning the mist persisted but a group of men had gone out into it to search. At length she had been found, towards evening, none the worse for her experience except for the fact that she no longer heard anything that was said. The mist, rain and wind of the long night had taken her hearing, left her deaf.

From then on she continued to do her work in the house and on the farm as before, spinning and knitting, milking, helping with turf and hay and anything else there was to be done, but her thoughts and memories were fixed, essentially, by a certain limit of time, that time until she could no longer hear what her family and friends and neighbours were saying. From then on, while their experience and thoughts and speech evolved, slowly, subtly, imperceptibly to them, into something they had not previously been, hers remained what they were before. So she became a kind of living remnant of a past time, a living repository of words and ways and thoughts that others had abandoned, stored up within herself, contained there but never to be expressed. A crude form of communication had developed between her and her closest family, a kind of mouthing of words and gesturing of hands and arms, and so small everyday things could be got across, but the big events remained unknown to her, except as she could deduce them from what she saw. Instead of coming up to date as faces and ways changed, however, she instead assimilated new things to old, thought that new faces were the old ones returned. Thus, as the world around her changed, she was left more and more in a personal world, the world of her own earlier life, and as those around her moved away from her they thought it was she who was moving away from them. In fact, she was the one who remained as she had always been.

Thus her speech had something strange about it, something unusual, because no longer usual, and as she sensed, without hearing it, that her words might not reach the person they were meant for, or might not be taken seriously by him, so she addressed herself partly to the world at large – to anyone and no one – and partly to herself. It was in that half loud, half muttering voice that she was saying something now about one of the cows.

'The old cow is for the country,' she announced. She began to pour the milk from pail to pitcher, then paused before she had actually poured any, the pail raised above the pitcher's lip. 'She'll be looking for the bull,' she said.

Peadar looked around at his sister. The old cow had calved something less than six weeks before. He had fixed the day in his mind because it was just two days after the hay had been carried in and built. He was expecting the old cow to come on, ready for the bull, but not as soon as this. Yet his sister had a way of knowing things beforehand, sometimes. It was hard to tell when she was imagining or remembering, and when she was talking about things that were going on now.

Resuming her pouring of the milk, she seemed to sense his scepticism, even though she had not looked his way. 'Aye,' she said emphatically. 'The old cow's for the country.' Then, almost without a pause, she took up a new subject. 'The black crows are on the hills,' she said. 'What are they after, them black crows? They must be after something.'

Peadar looked up. He himself had not seen the black crows. Was his sister imagining them, he wondered, or remembering them from another time, a time long past?

'Not them blue crows,' she continued, the adjective indicating the hooded crows that often appeared, black below but grey above – hence 'blue'. 'No, not them. The black crows.' Then once more she added the emphatic question: 'What they want?'

Peadar took the tea-pot from the fire with an old woollen sock wrapped around the handle, and poured the black tea out into the two mugs his sister had put out. He was rolling the question of the crows over in his mind, remembering his missing wether as he did so.

His sister went on, in a little voice as though singing or humming softly to herself, but talking nonetheless. 'Could be some sheep tumbled,' she said. 'Them black crows would have the eyes out – they would.' The last words were less an affirmation than a quiet comment to herself. 'They're the bad ones,' she added.

'Aye,' Peadar thought to himself, 'they're the bad article.' He took off his cap and rested it on his knee before he began eating. When he had finished his mug of tea, and two pieces of bread and butter, he crossed himself rapidly and replaced his cap on his head. Then he rose and fed his dog a breakfast like his own. That done, he took his stick from where he had left it leaning against the tall wooden cupboard, called his dog to follow him, and went out. He was thinking about the black crows he had not seen. He wondered if they were really there, and thought it possible that his sister had had a longer view of the hill from the cow-byre than he had had from the park. He walked towards the byre, then turned when he was still only half the way to it. He scanned the hill and the sky above it. The early October sun, though risen, had not yet appeared over the hill that faced his house across the valley from him, but its first beams were already falling on the very top of his own hill. He could not see anything on the hill but a few scattered ewes grazing quietly. There was nothing in the sky.

Turning, he went on to the byre and again looked back, once more running his eyes over the visible hill and sky. Almost at once he caught sight of the crows, two intensely black birds, rising and falling in the blue sky at the very top of the shoulder of the hill, rising and wheeling and swooping again, their wings immobile in the dive, then flapping and rising swiftly once more to wheel about one another high above the ground. As they did so they emitted a short hollow call that seemed to come from the depths of their throats, and that sounded ominously down to Peadar as he stood at the cow-byre below.

'It was them black crows. She knew it was them,' Peadar explained when he was recounting the event later to Wee Johnny, his neighbour on the facing hill slope across the narrow valley. 'Not them blue ones,' he said, 'but them real black ones, the ones with a glance on them' – indicating the brilliant sheen of the blue-black birds. 'You would see the light shine off them.' As he talked his arms and hands gestured the rising, wheeling, swooping flight of the birds, making visible their soaring movement to Wee Johnny. 'Those are the ones that make the nest in the spink, in under the top of the spink, you cannot get to them.'

The two men looked up involuntarily and away into the distance along the slope of the rising hills to where the dark cliff – the spink – rose steeply from the green slope, a cascade of dark rock that no farmer could climb or dog enter. 'Nor you cannot reach them with the gun, neither,' Peadar added. Both men knew where the nest was, tucked well in under the overhanging rock, high up and out of range of the gun.

'By Christ,' he went on, 'I says to myself, that's the wether. The wether is tumm'led, he's tumm'led over on his back.' He paused for emphasis. The two men, Peadar and Wee Johnny, were standing now discussing the event right on the spot outside the cow-byre where Peadar had first seen the crows, the same place, so they conjectured, where Peadar's sister had seen them earlier as she left the byre with the fresh milk. As they talked they heard the old cow low loudly, an annoyed reminder to the men, whose excited voices she heard coming through the rough wooden door of the byre, that she and the other cattle had not yet been put out to graze, were still tied in long past their accustomed moment to be turned out to the fresh aftergrass of the meadow.

When Peadar had seen the two crows, had watched for a moment the light of their glossy blue-black sheen, their graceful, ominous soaring flight, plummeting swoops and swift re-ascents into the sky, he marked the place where they

8

were in his mind and set out at a rapid walking pace to reach it. 'That's the wether,' he said to himself.

In a minute he had passed his park gate, and in another the house. His sister was in the doorway as he passed and a vague, quick gesture of her left hand towards the hill, towards the place where Peadar now knew the crows to be, was both a salutation and a comment. With the gesture she seemed to say again what she had said before in words.

In another minute Peadar was on the rough hill, climbing through the heather, leaping from one small knoll to the next. His dog stayed at his feet. They leapt a small stream that hurried downward through the steep bog. They passed a bank of turf along which stood a newly thatched stack of dry turf, the rushes of the thatch already faded to a pale yellowish green. Above him was a low outcropping of granite, a small replica of the massive black spink two miles further along the hills, the spink where the crows nested. He curved in his course to go around the rock as he climbed. It was only minutes since he had passed the house but already he was nearing the crest of the shoulder. The crows had disappeared from sight as he left the byre and the rise of the hill had interposed itself between him and them, but soon he would see them again.

As he came around the outcropping of rough granite he saw them, the crows, still rising and soaring and swooping as before, the deep hollow sound of their throated call descending to him as they did so. He had a sense of surprise, for he had thought they would by then have settled on to their prey, have pecked out the wether's eyes – or one eye at least, for the wether could protect one eye only by pressing that side of its head to the ground, leaving the other eye thus even more exposed to the crow's beak – and that he would find the wether with its fresh bright red blood staining the short black wool of its head and snout, a brilliant show of colour in a landscape that was all the brown of the bog, the rust of the coarse grass, the grey of the rock. He thought he would find the wether too late. Instead, the crows – 'them black crows, the real black ones' – were still soaring, still had not settled on their prey.

As he saw the crows, so, almost simultaneously, he saw the wether too. It was not tumbled, but was on its feet grazing not far from where he stood; and as he saw the wether his dog moved a few yards forward from his feet – for the dog too understood Peadar's thought – but Peadar called him in again to his foot. At the sound the wether looked up, a shred of long coarse red grass from its interrupted grazing hanging from the side of its mouth, its chewing motion suspended in the moment of its cautious curiosity. Then, seeing Peadar, it resumed its grazing again, moving forward a step as it did so.

Peadar looked for a moment at the wether. Clearly there was no harm on it. At once he thought of the crows again. Further on, a few hundred yards perhaps, he could see them rising and swooping still. Had a different sheep tumbled? His eye searched the bog beneath them but could detect nothing, no sign of whiteness that would locate for him a tumbled sheep. Nothing but the dull red-brown of the bog and its coarse grass and heather.

He walked on, less rapidly now, curving around a small round lake, walking then through an area of mires, high tufts of heathery ground interspersed with flat areas of grassless eroded turf, climbing continually as he walked until, near the top of the shoulder of the hill, he fixed his eyes once more as keenly as he could on the target the crows seemed to have as they rose and fell in the air. He was near enough now to see movement in the grass and to see that it was not a sheep. There was no wool. He stopped and stood still. There in the grass beneath the crows he saw what seemed to be his own yellow dog.

Quickly he looked down, half surprised to find the dog still at his feet. The dog too had stopped and was leaning forward intently, smelling the air with an audible drawing in of breath through its spread black nostrils. The dog, so much nearer the ground, could not yet see what Peadar, with his extra height, now saw clearly.

'What was it?' he asked rhetorically when he was telling the matter later to Wee Johnny. The question was a purely unnecessary one, as Johnny already knew the answer, but the delay in the narrative conveyed Peadar's own sense of suspension as his eyes slowly picked out a sight they had not seen before in years of walking about the hill, of looking after sheep. He paused, then answered his own question, his eyes going from narrow slits of puzzlement to the wideness of surprise. 'On'y the fox!' he said.

As Peadar, his dog at his feet snuffling the air more and more rapidly, looked on he saw with fascination this play of crows and fox. The fox – it was a large dog-fox and Peadar decided at once that it was the killer-fox he had heard about – was lying, half on its back, half on its side, waiting for the descent of the large black birds, then lunging, snarling and, jaws wide – Peadar thought he had never seen animal jaws open so wide – hurling himself viciously into the air. Then the broad black wings would flap hastily, and the crows, sounding quick uneasy cries of antagonism and alarm, would rise again, perhaps only a few yards up, before another quick swoop, perhaps higher. Given a moment's intermission, the fox quickly rolled to its feet and ran on, but not for far, as the crows quickly dove again to the attack. Then the fox was again on its back, claws lashing the air, jaws snarling.

Peadar had no idea how long he looked on. Probably only for seconds, he thought later, it could not have been a full minute, but the scene of animal conflict concentrated his senses and excluded all other thought, and so seemed a longer period of time, so intensely was it carried on. He knew at once that this was not the ordinary play he had sometimes seen foxes at. His mind went back to an early summer many years before when he had been sent, still a boy, high along the slowly rising slopes of Blue Stack itself, up above the long twist of falling white water he had heard called the Grey Mare's Tail, to search for a lost ewe and, attracted by the long view down the mountain valley from his high vantage point, looking down on the farms below, had suddenly seen a yellow fox much like the one before him now, playing and frolicking with the lambs that were grazing on the slopes beneath his eyes. The ewes ignored the playing fox, as though aware that there was no danger from him then, and went on grazing, but the lambs, running in files one after the other and imitating their own sudden leaps and twists into the air, leapt over the fox as he rolled on his back in their path, and themselves stood still to let him leap over them. Fox and lambs frisked and played, and the boy looked on, until without thought he suddenly heard himself whistling loudly. The grazing ewes stopped their grazing, the lambs ran to their mothers, the fox quickly disappeared, fleeing away and hiding himself as he did so behind small rises in the irregular ground.

Now, as he looked at this other scene, Peadar's mind went back to that earlier one. He knew that, just as the other had been a scene of play and high spirits in the early days of a coming summer, so the scene before him now was one of coming winter's deadly hardness. In another moment the conflict of fox and crows was broken by the rush of his own yellow dog into the midst of the action. With a barely audible little cry of eagerness, as though in anguish, the dog had rushed away from Peadar's feet and towards the place the fox and crows were trying one another. With a cry of alarm and annoyance the two birds rose and flew away, soaring easily across the high plain, seeming at times to fall sideways in their flight, then rising effortlessly again, upward and swiftly away. Quickly the fox rolled to its feet and began to flee, the dog in pursuit. The fox had been taken by surprise and the dog had almost got a grip on its hind quarters – had got a few loose red hairs instead. Now the two ran off, flight and pursuit, through the dull red bog, with intermittent snarls and shrieks of fear and hatred as they ran. Even Peadar, his eye used to discerning small details in the dull landscape, lost sight of them as they raced through it, only from time to time – all in the space of seconds – picking out a sudden noisy scuffle as fox and dog tangled in circling, rolling flight and then separated again into renewed flight and pursuit, following them more by sound than sight, not able to distinguish yellow dog from red fox even when he had sight of them, so alike were they in the colour of their fur and in their size.

The fox fled, by degrees of deviation, delayed by the snarling conflicts, in the direction of the granite outcropping Peadar had curved around to pass on his way up the hill. Peadar turned back and followed, walking quickly, rapidly, but taking his way cautiously nonetheless through the uncertain ground of the high bog. Arrived at the rocks, he saw his dog, small stains of fresh blood on its yellow fur, standing at a kind of crevice in the rock, leaning its weight forward, growling. The fox was trapped.

As Peadar approached he saw that the fox was trapped, but was also in safety. 'He had his ass in against the rock, you see,' he told Wee Johnny later. 'By Christ the dog could not come near him, he would snap him – he would finish him!' Peadar hesitated when he saw the two animals facing each other, paused and considered the situation. Then, slowly and planting each foot as he progressed with firm deliberation, slow and flat-footed but sure-footed as well, planting his stick before

12

him as he went, he approached the place where the fox had taken refuge. His intention was to hit the fox in its front legs with his stick, breaking the legs with the sudden swift blow. The helpless fox would then be ready for the kill.

He was several yards away when the fox, instantly seeing and taking advantage of the slight distraction of the dog's attention caused by his master's approach, raced away from the rock and towards Peadar, his jaws open for the snap. Peadar, taken by surprise, could barely begin to lift his stick. Only the yellow dog's quick lunge prevented the fox from reaching Peadar's leg, and again the flight continued, down the hill this time, the racing fox in front, the fiercely snarling, barking dog after him, and Peadar himself, running now and leaping in great excited arcs down the rough hill, brandishing his stick over his head instead of using it on the ground and calling out, in involuntary eagerness and pursuit, loud cries of encouragement to the dog. Only then, in that interval of swift movement in which he seemed to be in the air more than on the ground, did he perceive that the two animals were not as identical as he had thought, for he could make out then that the fleeing fox had dark, almost black ears, and his long tail, trailing straight out behind him, was redder and even bushier than the dog's yellow one.

Fox and dog and man were all heading now straight down the hill. Peadar saw the two animals pass the house and move towards the park. Judging quickly from the fox's size he was sure it would not get past the fence. It was too large to squeeze through. It would be turned by it and run along it, then possibly up the hill again. Or would it take refuge in one of the craws near the house – the chicken-craw, or the dog's own craw – putting its back to the wall to defend itself against approach? At that moment he saw his sister, apparently alerted by the wild, disarrayed fluttering flight of the hens, rush screaming from the house, the strident, harsh scream of the deaf, her stick in her hand, waving it before herself. In another instant he saw that he had been wrong about the fox, which had slipped deftly through a low hole under the lowest strand of wire.

'I knew then he'd been coming and going before that,' Peadar explained later. 'It be to be him pushed the sod out and made a path through – that's how the wether got out.' He knew too that the dog was too big to squeeze under the fence, even with the sod out beneath it, but before he had time to put the new question to himself the dog rose instead in his swift pursuit and easily leapt the highest wire of the fence, landing on the other side only inches behind the fox, which was just resuming its speed. As Peadar himself, third and last, climbed the fence at that same spot his mind had still enough awareness to perceive a tiny strand of short lamb's wool caught in a twist on the lowest wire – the tell-tale confirmation that the lamb had indeed got out that way. Then he became aware of his sister's piercing shriek once more, the shriek of the deaf.

'He'll kill the wethers! He'll kill the wethers!'

He saw running figures descending from the facing slope of the valley, and knew that, across the way, Wee Johnny and his family had heard the noise of dog and man and woman and come out of their house to see what it was. Geese and ducks and hens were chattering a noisy discordant chorus of alarm. Wee Johnny was running down his own hill, stick in hand, towards the bounds of Peadar's farm. The wethers on the park had stopped their grazing and gathered into a tight, uncertain flock, and Peadar saw the fox head directly into their midst, losing himself among them, in among the compact cover of crowding fleeces. The wethers turned towards the bottom of the park and the leaders began to run, the others following them, but at little, widening intervals so that the flock opened up as it moved down the slope. Reaching the bottom they wheeled about, ran along the bottom fence, then started upwards again. Peadar pulled himself to a stop and watched, his mouth open as if about to give a command to the dog, but without sound. The dog circled the flock of wethers, uncertain, catching sight of the fox for an instant, then as quickly losing him again. The wethers slowed and stopped. For a moment the action ceased.

'He'll kill the wethers!' He heard the shrieking voice again, and at that moment the yellow dog lunged into the flock. As he did so the fox reappeared, and raced upwards. Peadar had only just enough time to see him race to the two stone byres, the big cow-byre with its new coat of green thatch, and the small byre, its thatch black with age and rain, and disappear.

In a moment he had reached the byres. Fox and dog had disappeared. He examined the wooden doors of both byres, both doors improvisations of old pieces of wood recovered from some previous use and put together with nails and wire and twine, each with wide gaps at the bottom through which a fox could easily slip. He thought of the cattle tied in the larger byre and wondered if the fox had gone in among them to hide. He heard no sound of uneasiness. A quick look at the door of that byre reassured him. His sister had stuffed the cracks along the sides of the door with a wadding of rushes, and filled the open spaces below with tightly wedged hempen sacks themselves stuffed with more rushes. It was her way of protecting the cattle from the cold autumn drafts of approaching winter.

Peadar looked then at the small byre, speculating as he did so on the fox's course. Wee Johnny arrived and read Peadar's thought, repeating Peadar's own just-completed inspection of the cow-byre before returning to join him in scanning the door of the smaller building. Each man knew the other's thoughts. If the fox was inside, where was he hiding, and how could he be got at? The advantage was his.

Standing thinking these thoughts, they heard a low growl from within the byre, lengthening into a kind of angry, threatening whine.

'It's the dog,' Peadar said. 'The fox is in there!'

He went to the door, loosened the twine that held it closed, and opened it, catching sight as he did so of the dog crouching tensely, angrily, a few feet from the door itself, beside a high pile of sheared fleeces. That half of the byre was filled to the roof with the fleeces, but across from them was a lower pile, rising only half the way up the wall, and on top of it a large, round blackened iron pot, the bastible pot that had been used daily, years before when Peadar was young and his many brothers and sisters were still on the farm, to boil the quantities of potatoes on which the family fed. Out of use for many years it had been put down in the old byre to be out of the way. In the semi-darkness of the small interior it was the double glint of light from the fox's eyes that first let Peadar know where he was. Then he made out the rest of his form, crouching inside the pot, snout outward.

He closed the door and stopped for a moment to think. His hesitation was succeeded by anger, and anger brought determination. 'Watch yourself now, Johnny,' he said. 'He

15

would snap you.' But as he spoke the last words he stopped suddenly, hearing the sound of a quick, fierce clash in the byre, instantly followed by a rapid loud exhalation of breath, like an enormous sigh, and the bubbling, gurgling noise that he likened later to the sound of one of his own swiftly falling hill streams, then silence. He opened the door. In the dim light of the windowless interior he saw the yellow dog angrily shaking the fox's quivering, already lifeless body, his jaws firmly fixed into its throat. A rain of fresh blood had spattered the floors and walls, the highly piled white fleeces and the sides of the blackened iron pot with splashes and spots of red. The fox's legs and feet still moved rapidly back and forth, but frenetically and without strength, in a final, involuntary, useless imitation of living flight.

Peadar backed out and away from the spattering rain. 'It's the fox,' he commented to Wee Johnny. 'The dog finished the fox. The blood is skatin' out. It's comin' out of him in skates!' A sense of shock at the fox's sudden brutal death overcame his sense of victory and relief. Then he heard the old cow lowing loudly from within her own byre, the cow-byre that stood freshly thatched across from Peadar's 'wee byre'. Peadar laughed – a laugh of relief and recollection all in one. 'She wants to get out,' he said. 'I forgot about them when I saw the crows. I never thought to put them out.'

It was not yet midday, but it was late for the cattle. They were anxious to be out on the grass. Peadar leaned his stick against the green stones of the byre, loosed the bit of rope that held the door shut, removed the rushes and the rush-filled sack, and then, bowing his head to enter through the low opening, went into the byre and untied the two cows and two calves tethered in their stalls. He stood back while they made their quick way through the door and out. As they passed the door of the small byre the old cow reared slightly, getting the scent of the newly dead fox, and let out a short nervous snort. Otherwise the cattle seemed unaware of the event.

But as they filed through the narrow gap which Wee Johnny had opened into the park, Peadar stopped and stood again to observe them for a minute, his eye caught by the strange behaviour of the old cow, who herself had stopped to sound from curving, extended throat and widely opened snout a long deep horn-blast of dissatisfaction, and then, without putting her snout to the grass, leaped about as though a young and frisky animal again. Peadar looked on in surprise, and with amusement. Looking over at Wee Johnny again, 'By Christ,' he said, 'she was right. The old cow's for the country!'

THE SCYTHE

The bones of the body hinge and joint in swivels and sockets, the limbs move in arcs and circles, long regular curves and courses, graceful easy movements. The tool's handle extends the reach of the arm, describes a larger arc, a stronger force. At the end of the wooden snad the delicate crescent of steel scythe mows with sharpened mouth the grass before its sweep, the metal curve a precise expression of the body's jointed movements. But to swing the scythe? And before that, to sharpen it?

'Not every man can sharp the scythe, but if it's in your hand to do it, you will.'

I was in a hurry to sharpen the scythe, to cut the long heavy rushes that were meant for thatch, to thatch the old dry-stone byre that had been saved, just in time, if only for a time, from the inevitable sequence of decay, rot and dilapidation that is the final history of every rough-thatch house and byre and shed. And why did the byre mean so much to me, its salvation so important? Antithesis to everything prized in my world; not efficient, not easy. The roof itself a labour of thousands of bits, thousands of individual stalks of rush laboriously cut by hand, gathered then by hand, cleaned of the clinging grass at their base, arranged then in neat, fat sheaves, thick and heavy green bundles with half their contents running one way, half the other – seed-top to base and base to seed-top – the whole tied with a rope made then for just that purpose, a coil of strands of those same rushes, itself twisted upon itself in a final tight cincture. The hundreds of sheaves carried then, with their thousands of green stalks of rush, to the byre and laid on the roof in a neat, interlocking texture of combed green roof, a tiling, tiles in structure yet so harmoniously interworked that no seam or join could be detected, the thousands of rushes working together in one smooth and purposeful whole: the thatch roof. And it, as I learned afterwards, watching it, was first green, then quickly faded to a rich and warm colour of fresh straw, followed later by a loss, a dissolution, of the warm tones, leaving finally a faded, pale straw, greying by degrees until once more the slow but continuous work of rain and mist would crevass the thatch with deepening areas of darkness, moist channels where water would lodge, never fully dried, drawing to itself the inevitable garish green moss, the first blades of grass, clumps later, until the process began again from the beginning. The thatch roof, with its cycle of freshness and age, decay and resurrection and another freshness, was itself like the longer, slower succession of generations that lived themselves through around it, the generations of living things, animals, men, ever ageing and decaying, dying, ever-renewed in replicas of themselves.

But I saw and thought none of this then. Before me was a problem: to cut the rushes. I did not see the rush as my ally, the useful material of my roof. It was the heavy, dark weed that devastated my fields. Not yet had I learned of the sayings of the oldest farmers, that a good field without rushes was not a good field. I had not yet seen the young sheep sheltering on the bleak and treeless slopes, behind the heavy rush clumps from the chilling, unimpeded winds; nor had I yet discovered the impenetrable cleverness by which the ewe settled her young lamb neatly into the middle of a rush-bush on a stormy, hail-stony day; nor did I know that the thick grass growing up in the heart of the rush, shunned by sheep and cattle during the summer and fall months, the months of abundant growth and grass, would be thus preserved, a kind of uncut hay, to help fodder those same sheep and cattle through the barren months of winter; only later did I see the sheep in thick falls of snow wandering from rush-bush to rush-bush, chewing into the rushes themselves, transforming them thus from ugly weed to life-preserving fodder. Of all that I knew nothing. The rush was only the enemy of neat greenness, of the well-managed meadow – enemy, that is, until cut and gathered and transformed into a roof, made useful.

But to sharpen the scythe: I was in a hurry to cut the thatch, the scythe was only the implement, the means, and my modern mind was fixed not on the means, but on the end. Was not the end, in my world, the only justification of the means, themselves unimportant? And so in my haste I left the implement improperly sharpened and broke the rushes with heavy, smashing blows instead of cutting them. But I was unaware of that, too, until later.

'Take your time and get all done,' he said. It took time, too, to learn that the statement was also a syllogism, a logical proposition, that I would have stated differently, beginning with a conditional *if*, transforming the *and* into a sequential statement of result.

'What about the two caddies?' he asked, the question itself a transition to another statement.

What *about* the two caddies? I thought to myself. Am I supposed to know about them? Has something happened I should know about but don't? But I barely knew that a 'caddy' was a boy, and the strange intonations of the speech around me were only caught and unravelled with effort. Hence I listened the more intently to the sense as well.

'The two caddies that were going home, and had the river to cross,' he said, 'and the river in flood, from the rains, you see. There be to be heavy rains that time. And they could go around by the bridge, if they would take their time, but they made out they would cross by the wee stones were in it. They would save a minute, you see, crossing on the wee stones, and not go by the bridge. And the flood took them with it then, and they were seen no more.'

He paused, and I waited, and then he continued.

'And that day year, the old man was in the kitchen, and he said to the mother, "And if they would go around by the bridge they would have plenty of time ahead of them yet."'

It was a story to ponder, a tale to fill out a lesson, a fable that came back to the simple task of the sharpening of the scythe. But, even granted patience, how was it to be done? Men had paused and seen me at the work, strangers to myself, and stopped and offered assistance. One had taken the scythe in hand and, setting the base of the wooden snad firmly against the ground at his foot, inspected the blade with knowing consideration. The fingers of his left hand investigated the condition of the edge. Taking hold of one of the handles, he held the scythe lightly balanced in his right hand, looking at it and then at me, deciding whether or not the fitting and angle of the blade had been correctly done to suit the user. Then resting the point of the vertically held blade against the ground, the snad a diagonal descending from blade-base to the ground, he took hold of the gently tapered blue stone and began the steady, rhythmical sharpening of the scythe.

'Not everyone can sharp the scythe,' he said, and bent his head and body over the blade, setting his feet apart in a firm stance, the hard stone whirring softly as it slipped across the smooth face of the metal, the arc of its movement duplicating the arc of the scythe, as the scythe did that of the human hand, whose own curving movement was a vector of many joints and parts. The stone hummed, and the sharpening went on rhythmical and regular for what seemed to me a long while, in several phases dedicated each to a different section of the blade's length, until finally the scythe was lifted and the sharpener, standing erect, slid the stone back and forth with rapid movements above and below the ever more gleaming pointed tip of the blade. Then again the visual and tactile examination followed, and a final honing in reverse order, until at last the condition of the scythe was thought perfect, ready for the heavy work of cutting. Putting down the sharpening stone and balancing the scythe lightly again in his right hand and advancing to the dense growth of rushes he bent his knees slightly, inclined his body forward, put his left hand to the other handle, and then he swung the scythe lightly, gently, in an easy and effortless arc into the cluster of rushes before him. The hum of the metal blade entering the rushes and slicing through them echoed as it did so the whirring sound of the stone before it. The rushes fell, their lengths landing in neat, orderly lines.

He straightened up. 'There it is for you now,' he said, laying the scythe gently on the ground. 'Go easy with it, very easy. You have no call to smash and hammer. Let the scythe do the work.'

But it was a hard lesson to learn. For me, hard work could only be hard, the scythe was a tool, an instrument of labour, and the rush was the enemy. It added up, all of it, to effort, not ease.

And so, laboriously, I cut the rushes for the byre, and the byre was thatched, and my first lesson with the scythe was past. I would find it hard to say now whether or not I had learned anything. Perhaps before learning can come there is an inevitable phase of effort and failure and blindness, an effort that leads to no more than the exhaustion of ignorance.

But when it was time to mow the hay late in the following summer the scythe came into question again. The hay of the high hill meadow was too far from towns, too low on the priority list of available mechanical mowers, to be cut in any way but by hand, by the scythe. And so the investigation began again, the research and experimentation into the use of the scythe. And throughout it was to me a vast and complex mystery of interlocking parts, inexplicable, a strange talent that a man was born with, but could not teach or learn, a talent akin to the talent of the creative artist, born into him, never acquired, never passed on through any channel but the transmitted blood of replicating generations, the replicated hands and arms, limbs, bones and joints, and movements. Those who lacked the skill could only discuss it in puzzlement, those who possessed it could not explain it. They could demonstrate it. But if the rest of us could not perceive the essence of their demonstration?

'I sit and watch him mow,' a young farmer said, looking across the valley towards the farm of his older neighbour, 'and he puts down those acres of hay – it's a big park, you know – and I see, somehow, he's not working at all. He must have a wild edge on the scythe.'

I looked across the valley to the curved, crouching figure on the other slope, and perceived then what I had been told to perceive, the light and easy movements, seemingly without effort, as the scythe entered the tall thick grass.

'A wild edge on the scythe,' he had said. But how to get it?

At the back of the blade runs a heavy ridge, the steel itself curved upward and backward. That ridge, he said, was the guide-line for the stone. Run it along that and the angle of the stone as it moved would fall correctly along the blade, correct to the edge, backward and forward, steady against the ridge of steel, to bring the blade to its right edge. Pressure was important, or rather lightness. 'No more than the weight of the stone itself,' I was told. A young man skilled in mowing took my scythe from me and tested the edge. 'You've turned the edge,' he said, disappointment in his tone.

It was the curse of the beginner, the mark of the inept, to turn the edge, to leave a thin rough bevel, no more than the fineness of the finest wire. Then the scythe cut well for a dozen strokes, perhaps a score, and then its keenness failed again.

And there were kinds of stones, as I discovered at last. Old men preserved stones carefully in rags of cloth and remembered still at what fair they had bought them and for what price. Seven miles from us was a quarry famous for its stone. I was directed there, and listened to the stonecutter, old then and sitting by his hearth, praise the stone that had gone in building blocks to all parts of the world, to participate in mansions and monuments and even the palaces of kings, the stone on which he had carved so many Celtic crosses and designs. But he corrected my information. The stone of his quarry was not right for the scythe. When he was young he had collected stones suitable for sharpening from the river-bed and had carried creels-full of them to the fairs, selling them there for a few pennies apiece. 'Twelve miles to Glenties, fifteen to Ardara, with the creel of stones on your back. Oh, aye, we never missed a fair. And we never brought a stone home again, all were sold.'

But even before the finding of the stone another step was to be taken, not foreseen until it occurred. It came by accident, unexpected, not from a mowster, but from the taxi-driver transporting me home, the scythe, a new one and newly fitted by the smith, tied to the car roof-rack. For that was another ritual, another step in the work and rhythm of the scythe. As autumn approached the consignment of new scythes appeared in the shops, point down, tang up, in a wooden cask or barrel, to be lifted by the tang and examined by knowing hands, scraped along the stone floor for signs of a musical ring, the witness of true-tempered steel, held out at arm's length for sighting along the edge to determine by eye the correctness of the form and forging. Purchased at last, the blade and the wooden snad, similarly inspected, were taken to the forge and there the smith, the bellows of his shop roaring a searing heat into the black fuel of his fire, fashioned iron spikes to take the wooden handle-grips, iron rings and wedges to clasp the scythe itself securely against the snad, and then, carefully measuring by look or glance the user, he determined the precise placing of each handle, the precise angle of the blade, its precise pitch as well, hammering the glowing tang to shorten or lengthen it and turn it by just the required amount. The scythe, assembled thus

23

individually to suit the size and dimensions of the individual mower, balanced easily in the hand, swung in the perfectly appropriate arc, did its work without effort.

'A good mowster uses only the force of his arms, at his dead ease. If you feel it in your back you're doing it wrong.'

Only the strength you would use to swing the scythe in air, that was all that was to be used even against the obstacle of grass or rushes! It was a hard lesson to learn, harder perhaps than smashing the scythe against its object, and first it was necessary to sharpen the scythe to such an edge. And then, by chance, the taxi-driver had given the key. 'When you get a new scythe first,' he said, 'it's a good thing to lay a straight file against it and bring it to an edge.'

But another farmer, consulted, disagreed – disagreed in anger. It would destroy the goodness of the blade, he said.

Oddly, then, the sharpening of the scythe had become a communal debate, if only within my own perceptions, the debaters not physically present in hall or theatre to assert and contradict and answer one another, but answering individually the assertions I carried and compared from member to member of the community, the questions and tentative answers working only within my own mind and thoughts and the trials and errors of the scythe. Progress was inevitable – I see that now. I got better with the scythe, and learned more about all farming as I did so; but always the temptation was strong to make up for the decreasing sharpness of the edge by swinging with harder and harder force. Then, by a law of physics that even I remembered, the force exerted against the grass or rush exerted itself in turn back upon the user, upon his scythe and himself, demonstrating itself graphically one day in a scythe neatly snapped in two at the tang. The young man on the county road-crew, who had been sent ahead of the others to cut the rushes that grew in the middle of the road in preparation for a new gravelling, was not surprised, and looked reproach, but only said: 'What did you expect?'

So I knew that I was far from the goal. At least one essential element was missing from my art, and I was trying to compensate with force for lack of skill, or craft. And then at last I began to understand, and abandoned the goal, for a while, and turned my mind to the means alone. Then followed long hours of experiment, and others of observation. Gradually I learned to perceive, even while I worked, even before I tried to use the sharpened tool, the angle of the stone, the pressure of my hand, the fineness of the edge, and in the long hours and days I spent shaking out freshly mown hay for others I stopped my work when they stopped theirs and stood observing then, from whatever angle to the mowster chance had put me in, the movements with which he sharpened his scythe, his stance, posture, gesture.

My friend and I had driven up to the centre of the county to visit another friend who was in the general hospital. When we were leaving, had left our friend in his ward and were threading our way back along the empty corrridors towards the open world again, my companion decided that we would visit another friend of his, across the road, in the other hospital, long confined for a less tangible, less treatable illness. It was the hospital people meant when they said a man, or woman or child, had gone 'through the gap'. The *gap*, I discovered, was a real pass high in the hills that carried the only road leading into the centre of the county from where we were, and I heard men use it to mean only that, and no more, that they were going thirty or forty miles north for a day's business. But it was used in this other sense, too, and to me it seemed an apt metaphor for the flight from sanity, accidental or designed, that narrow gap between the sane and insane minds through which a man may pass almost without perceiving the passage, the gap so hard to find again for the return journey.

I was reluctant to go in, for I had heard rumours of violence, nothing good or redeeming had yet reached my ears, but my friend insisted.

'You'll like to meet him,' he had said.

He appeared suddenly at the end of an upstairs corridor, a large man, tall and broad, and then in the first instance of meeting more like a city-man in his dress and appearance, his neat suit, his fresh shirt and carefully knotted tie, close-shaven cheek and barbered hair, than a farmer. Involuntarily, against my own will, I looked for signs of insanity, trying to repress and hide my looking both from myself and from him. We sat in a small triangle of plain wooden chairs pulled together in the empty dining-room, and talked. The two old friends talked, asked and answered about other common friends, and then slowly turned to farming talk, and I perceived as they talked a progression of seasons and labours, the one ruddy and firm, rough in dress and look, talking of his current work, of everyday, the other, surprisingly like a city-man in looks, well-groomed, pale, talking from memory but participating gladly in the recollection of the farm routine.

Then he turned to me and spoke as if he had long known me, although we had never met before. And then on again to farming, and then he told me, calmly, quietly, that he had worked hard at his farm, too hard, and that he had been alone, and hard things happen to a farmer who is alone. He cannot see to everything. He talked about moments of depression on the farm, and I, from recollections of similar times, when work had been too great and help too scarce and the multiple burdens had seemed too oppressive for a single strength, listened to him talk not as one strange to the experience, peering through an unfamiliar gap, but as one would listen to the everyday routine of another farmer's work, the known experience of another's life.

Looking at me, quiet and calm, his eyes on mine, 'There were times,' he said softly, 'when I was mentally unstable. I lost my sanity. So I was confined in here.'

I could not grasp the significance of what he had said – rather, of the fact that he had said it. I understood, and yet refused to understand; but perhaps through my mind ran a question that I refused to hear. Quickly I turned the talk back to farm matters and, inevitably, to the scythe.

And then he talked about the scythe, briefly, but clearly, his talk a strange combination of gathered experience and clear exposition, a collaboration of work and words that I had not encountered before, and suddenly I saw that in his explanation he had gathered and ordered the conflicting ideas and methods that had already gathered themselves without order within my mind in the long, unresolved debate.

It was a moment of clarity. I looked into the calm eyes, his modest but steady gaze, glanced again at his rounded shoulders. I said something, made some remark again about the scythe, about the sharpening of scythes, but my thoughts, inward, were other thoughts. Looking at this man who had just acknowledged his own madness to me, I was suddenly addressing myself, my own self, and all my generation, condemning myself, and them, for the outward show of sanity, for the tacit assumption of sanity, for the refusal to acknowledge our own madness, instead plunging blindly on to eat and consume and destroy the earth we lived on, in greed, and need for ease, and lack of courage to face a harder life – alone perhaps, without comfort perhaps – while this man sat, confined, calm, having confessed his own madness to himself and so having achieved a sanity – or so I thought, a greater achievement than any of ours. In that instant I thought of the ancient philosopher who boasted of wisdom only because, he said, he had learned that he was ignorant; but the man before me – did he not surpass the philosopher when through the knowledge of his madness he had become sane?

I sharpened my scythe then in a different way, and as I worked I was aware of a craft, a single element of craft but wonderful nonetheless, that had grown through many conversations and trials and contradictions, a gathering of information from many sources, a kind of intellectual debate, yet at once a creative effort, a balancing finally of mental and physical striving, an ultimate harmony of the two, combining and working together, the keystone and resolving thought coming to me when least expected, from the mouth of the least-sought man.

Finally I set off to use the new and hardly acquired skill, not without a certain desire to demonstrate its acquisition. The old people, high in the mountain valley, still had kept their original roof of thatch, never had yielded to the temptation to replace the laborious but valuable insulation of their home-grown thatch by the easier, inferior foreign tin. Carefully I remembered the instructions, the rules, the slowly gathered data in the long and undiplomaed course I had constructed for myself, resisted the urge to make the work hard, disciplined myself to mow 'at my dead ease'. Long and patiently I bent over the scythe, bringing the edge to its true razor-sharpness, rising then and letting it balance easily in my hand, swinging it gently then into the clump of rushes, an easy, slicing swing, held at a perfect angle, entering the rushes in a perfect arc, slicing, a true extension of the bones and joints of limbs, an extension of strength, an extension of mind. And as I worked the work became not hard but easier, until, when the rushes had been gathered in sheaves and the sheaves in a high pile at the gable of the thatched house, I could see at last the satisfaction of the old people, their gladness at the thought of yet one more phase of freshness for the thatched roof.

But it was not until I was leaving, the sun already behind the hill to the west, that I understood at last this long story, and heard its final part. The old man came out to the gravel path then and stopped me as I was going away, to thank me for the work.

'Thank you for the work,' he said, 'and big luck on you till you be better paid. Big luck on you till you be better paid. And I'll tell you a story about that.'

I stopped and turned towards him, and smiled, for I sensed the joke that was only a prelude to the true payment which I would refuse, when it was offered, and then reluctantly accept. But to me, at any rate, the words I was about to hear were more important, and so, smiling, I listened carefully.

'There was a man living over in your townland one time,' the old man said. 'Con was his name, and he was over on that farm next to yours. And he used to be away working at houses. He was a wild good worker, and everyone wanted Con, and they were well pleased with him, and with the work, and when he was done working, "Big luck on you," they would say, "big luck on you till you be better paid." Big luck on you, till you be better paid. That was the thanks. So Con says, "Pay-day never come, so Con quit working." Pay-day never come, so Con quit working.'

The old man paused, then resumed. 'Big luck on you, till you be better paid. And pay-day never come, so Con quit working.'

I laughed softly and started to leave. My final lesson with the scythe had been a lesson in history – world history, personal history.

'Well,' he said, 'big luck on you till you be better paid.'

BROCK

'A small brown dog, the colour of a badger. And you would hear no voice from him. Nor the sheep would not scare before him, the way they will before a black dog, when he was so like the badger, you see, for they'll not scare before the badger neither.'

Paddy Rua's kitchen was a mass of irregular stone wall, built long before mortar or plaster was known in the Donegal hills, but smoothed to gentle undulations by generations of whitewash, topped above by the arch of crude roof, the rough-hewn timbers and wattles softened and darkened by equally long generations of smoke from the low stone hearth. The storms that warned of their approach by sending the smoke adversely down the stone chimney to fill the low kitchen had coated the wood with a dark, oily soot and so preserved it from worm and rot. Some thought the soot had preserved the people of the house too, with its penetrating astringency, and Paddy Rua, somewhere in his nineties, could still rise from his stool beside the hearth to go out the kitchen door and look over his land and as much of his hill as could be seen, in the ancient manner of farmers scanning the ground to satisfy himself that all was in order, that cattle and sheep were grazing in their accustomed manner and haunts, and that 'nothing strange' had interrupted the normal, safe course of animal life on his land. But mostly he sat close to his hearth and its piled turf, turning first one side and then the other to the glowing heat, and recollecting a time before any trace of modern life had been felt in the hills. By agreement Paddy Rua was in his nineties, though some thought he was near the beginning of them, while others put him well further on. A young valley farmer, careless of the nice discretion of the hills, had asked him, and Paddy Rua had thought for a while before speaking.

29

'Damned if I can mind.'

He looked at the fire.

'Damned if I can mind it now. It be to be in the parish register, for Father Cleary there, God rest him, he was there that time, and he looked it out. That was the time the pensions first come to this country, and he looked it out to see when was I baptised and was I the age for the pension. But damned if I can mind what year ago that were.'

A long discussion followed, with ample intervals for recollection and consideration, between Paddy Rua, sitting by the hearth, and his wife, Mary, a generation younger and ceaselessly shuffling back and forth between hearth and kitchen table as she put bread on to roast above the fire or added fresh water to the kettle or, for want of other work, simply swept the red ashes of the burnt turf back into the hearth, tirelessly interjecting brief affirmative commentaries on Paddy's words – 'Aye, caddy, you're right there,' was the usual formula, for even at Paddy's great age she still called him 'caddy' in sign of approval and affection – and their son, Briney Paddy Rua, another generation younger still, the real 'caddy' of the house, the human power source for any heavy work. Their voices contrasted by turns, the sound of the wind in Paddy's but the mist and rain in his son's, and in his wife's throat the thin twitter of a bird. But the only conclusion of their deliberations was that 'it be to be twenty year or more since the pensions come out first', and nothing more was said about Paddy Rua's age. One thing only was certain, and that was that every trace of the fiery redness of hair that had given Paddy Rua his name had yielded to a perfect, silvery white.

'Aye,' he said, going back to his recollection of the brown dog. '*Het* was a bad winter, you would say, when the snow lay about the streets in wreathes for months and weren't gone from the hills until summer. By Christ the sheep got it hard that year. There was ones lost in the snow in the high hills beyont, and not got at all until spring, and then only the horns got, and bits of fleece. And there would be more lost too, oh loads more, only a man had a good dog to take them to him.' To which remark there were more affirmations, both from the wife and the son, who simply shook his downcast head slowly and commented, 'Oh, aye, indeed, you want a good dog with the sheep.'

30

A glowing turf on the hearth dislodged itself from the rest of the fire and tumbled on to the flagstones at Paddy's feet. He took up the black iron tongs that stood propped in a corner of the hearth near him and began a delicate rearrangement of the brick-like chunks of turf, until the integrity of the fire had been restored. Then he rose and went to the door, and looked up towards the hills.

'There's a name on every part of the hill. A name in Irish, that a man would know where he was, and if he saw a sheep lost there, or something else like that, he could tell the man that lost it, and him go straight to where it were, and take it with him.'

He stood on the 'street', as he called the level clay ground before his house, and looked over the land before him.

'That hill there now, away from us there, *Cruk Mian* we call that, the Fine Hill. And that big rock you see, that's *Caricka Keena*, the Rock of the Fog, the green fog that grows about the hills. And the high hill there beyont the river, that's *Ben Bwee*, the Yellow Hill. And there above, above the path that we go out and in, that's *Ben Doo*, is the name that's on it in Irish, and in English they call it the Black Spink. *Het*'s the bad article.'

He looked upwards along the steeply sloping green hill that rose behind his house to the uneven mass of vertical black rock that capped it. High, dark, irregular, a looming shadow of rock crossed by strips of green that attracted sheep and drew them, at times when grass was scarce, by gradual degrees further and further in to the sharp, uneven cliff face, until they found themselves isolated, marooned on a narrow ledge of rock with no way out, none at least that they could find. One who knew sheep could perceive, even from the river-valley five hundred feet below, their near-sighted perplexity as they stood, shifting their stance only intermittently, waiting as though in patient expectation of an opening to appear, of further grazing before them to lead them on, then returning to an examination of the scanty well-picked sward under their feet – but mostly simply standing, expectant, patient.

It happened two or three times a year, this catching of sheep in a natural trap. Almost always it was the year-old ewes – the 'yirrols' – that got caught, sheep in the first part of their lives that had not yet learned to be sufficiently wary. And then the sheep farmers looked upwards from the river valley, calm, betraying no anguish or sense of loss. That was felt inwardly, not expressed. To count the loss aloud would only be to add discouragement to damage. But mostly it was hard, or impossible, to get the sheep out again.

'Excepting a man had a good dog could take them out of it,' Briney Paddy Rua said over his shoulder as he sat at the small wooden table in the far corner of the kitchen, facing the wall and taking his bread and tea. Above him, in the spaces between the wattles and the earth sods of the roof itself tobacco-darkened clay pipes were wedged, and two pairs of wool-shears hung from wooden pegs, their points downwards. On the floor near the table stood a tall, unpainted wooden churn. Pinned to the wattles of the roof above the hearth was a Brigid cross woven of green rushes. Briney filled his mouth with bread, tearing it off with a sideways forceful motion of his head, and took a sip of tea.

'That brown dog now,' he said, 'he would take a sheep out of the spink, and do it handy. You would see him handle them quiet, very quiet. You would enjoy to see him do it.'

Paddy Rua looked over at his son for a moment.

'Did you know that dog?' he asked. 'I thought that dog was before your time. By God, I was only a young caddy myself when I had that dog, younger nor you are now, I doubt.'

Briney finished eating his mouthful.

'Well, I didn't know him,' he said. 'But I often hear tell, you see.'

'Aye,' Paddy resumed. '*Het* was a dog, Brock. That's the Irish on *badger*. You see, when he was so like the badger, we called Brock on him. And he was very biddable, and quiet. It was the nature of the dog, you see, that he would come when you whistle him and walk quiet at your foot. Nor he would not catch any sheep neither, nor do them no harm.'

'He was a great dog indeed,' Mary interjected, twittering as she poured more tea from an old aluminum tea-pot into Briney's cup. 'Aye, caddy, he was a good one.'

'Thon was the dog could take the yirrols from the spink,' Briney added.

'He could!' Paddy Rua said with emphasis, his eyes beginning to glow with the evoked past.

'By God, there are plenty of good dogs now can do nothing in the spink,' Briney went on. 'For there is Charley Fetey's big yellow dog that's as good as any dog these parts, would take

32

the sheep to you as nicely' – Briney smiled and held his arm in a gentle, horizontal arc before him – 'and put them in the yard for you, and you doing nothing only standing looking on. But if the same dog would come to the spink, you would have work to get him out, you would have to carry him out of it yourself, for he can do nothing in it, only stand. He would be afeared, you see.'

'Aye,' Paddy said. 'I often seen that. But the brown dog was afeared of nothing, and would go in along them wee ledges, and as quiet' – he gestured tranquillity with his hands – 'and turn the sheep, the way they would make their way out again, quiet, very quiet. Many's the sheep he took out of that Black Spink. And in that bad winter when the snow lay about the streets in wreaths until spring he was in it four or five times – he was! – and he saved a pile of sheep. You would see the wee brown dog that clear on the white snow. Back and forth, back and forth, until the sheep was out. Sheep that were in it and would be starved with the cold, standing there and nothing to get, they would starve, you see, only he put them out of it. A wee brown spot back and forth on the white snow.'

Briney crossed himself rapidly after finishing his tea, replaced his cap on his head with a twist of the peak from side to front that settled it firmly in place, pushed his chair back, and rose from the table. 'It's a pity no pup were saved off him,' he said. Then he took his stick and walked through the kitchen door, mindful of some routine obligation calling him away. He had heard about the brown dog before, probably more than once, and was too young and vigorous to sit by the fire listening to accounts of what was past when there was present work to do.

Paddy Rua watched him go out, his own eyes watery and slightly dim as they turned from the darkness of the kitchen to the brighter light coming in through the open door.

'No pup,' he echoed. 'There were no pup saved off him.'

The soft rumble of a tractor, the sound rising as though filtered through the hill air from the valley below, caught his attention for a moment. He turned his face back to the fire, to his recollections of the past, of a time when it was a man's work to walk the rough hills in every weather and see to his sheep, and no machine noise, no whine of car or lorry or rumble of tractor, had ever interrupted the natural sounds of the hill valley, nor marred with their exhaust the soft and everchanging smells of the sloping ground. His mind and thoughts went back to those times easily, and he remembered and spoke of a way of life that was gone, of people and of animals that had died half a century before, or longer, and of beliefs that had lapsed. Life had been different then, lived differently, seen differently. Across the hills there had wandered a race of tall, vigorous men who had shared with their half-wild sheep and cattle more than just a habitat, had shared as well a way of being, had shared some of the wildness, even to the wildness of the strange beasts that were unknown only a few miles further east in the tame and disciplined valleys of the dairy farmers: the water-horses, the winged eels, the sword-nosed water-dogs. He had known many things that were hardly and only reluctantly talked of to anyone from beyond the fringe of the hills.

'Everything's away entirely forebyes what it used to be,' he commented on his own recollections.

At last his thoughts went back to the brown dog, Brock. The dog had been brought, a pup of a few weeks, over the hills from the glen beyond. He had arrived one night at the farm kitchen in the tweed pocket of a hill farmer's jacket, carried over the hill on the chance that he might be wanted somewhere. Placed on the kitchen flagstones, he was looked at carefully and curiously for a few moments, he himself looking back quietly at faces never seen by him before.

'A nice wee pup,' was the first comment from one of the group around the hearth.

'Aye,' came the reply. 'He has a wise look about him.'

So, on the ground of his wise look, the 'wee brown pup' stayed, and was known as just that, 'the wee brown pup', until someone noticed that the sheep never shied from him when he came near them, but always turned away from him slowly, scarcely even interrupting their grazing. 'It's because he's like the badger,' an old man – a man old when Paddy Rua was young – had pointed out, 'for the sheep'll not scare before the badger neither.' From that Brock got his name, and had quickly taken to following at Paddy Rua's feet – the brown dog with the red-haired man, as the neighbouring farmers remarked, amused at the sight of the small pup following in untaught obedience the tall, thin shepherd. 'The dog's hair brown like the badger,' one of them said, 'and the man's red like the fox.'

Paddy Rua made no effort to train the young dog, but when sheep were being moved or brought together his hands and body spontaneously gestured and spoke in the visual language of the working of sheep. The dog learned without being taught, until one day he moved in a long arc away from Paddy Rua's foot, slowly and quietly out beyond the sheep, rounding them up and taking them away from men and dogs and under his own control.

'He went off then,' Paddy Rua remembered, 'and he took them sheep with him. We were watching to see what would he do, and where would he go. It was the back of *Ben Bwee*, and the dog went away from me and left me on the back of the hill, and I did not see him more until I come down to the house here. And him sitting there, and had the sheep put in the yard and all, and him sitting in the gap, keeping them in. He put them in the yard his self, and kept them there. I knew then I had a good dog.'

Paddy Rua soon found that he was right. The dog was a good one, and loyal to the man. Refusing to work for anyone else, he would never leave Paddy's heels. In the worst of storms he stayed with him until all the sheep were seen, or brought together, and when winter blizzard winds blew the snow into deep drifts in the hollows of the northern slopes the dog still remained loyally with the man, leaping and almost swimming his way across or through the drifts, his fur powdered with snow, drops of half-frozen water gathered about his face and nose, blinking into the driving wind, but always staying as long as there was work with the sheep. But most impressive of all was to see the small brown form of the dog climb the snow-covered hillside that led to the Black Spink, slowly ascend and cross over and above the spink to return, slowly, to the difficult narrow ledges beyond and then, entering one of the ledges, to persuade the trapped sheep to turn and make their way slowly out again.

'Thon was a loyal dog,' Mary interjected, as she took the lid from the iron oven that hung above the fire and peered in to see the condition of the roasting bread.

'And a very gentle one,' Paddy added. 'The only one thing would put him wild was the thunder. He could not abide it, and when he found the rattle of the thunder he was away, and you would not see him more that day. And another was the gun. If there would be hunters about, the dog was away with the first rattle of the gun, up in some wee holes in the spink, hiding until they be gone, till he would come out again.'

'But sure plenty dogs be's that way,' Mary interposed.

'Aye,' Paddy answered. 'Some does.'

It was the dog's alarm at thunder and shots that started the trouble. Paddy had a gun himself, a long-barrelled, straight-stocked muzzle-loader, with which he used to shoot rabbits and hares or, when luck brought him close enough, an occasional fox. Seeing the dog's fear, he used the gun less often, and when unrest began about the country and it was known that searching raids were being made even on farms in the hills he took the gun high up the sloping hill-side and left it in a low rock cave at the foot of the Black Spink. A veil of glossy dark ivy leaves hid the opening from sight.

But one day the first tractor came to the hill valley and with it a frightening collection of engine noises, louder, more astonishing, than either thunder or gunshots. It was a new experience for the inhabitants, and Paddy Rua was not very surprised to find his dog gone. Nor did Brock return for three days.

'He's up in one of them wee holes up under the spink,' Paddy remarked to the old people who had expressed their uneasiness about the dog's long absence. 'He'll soon quit that and come down, when he finds the tractor away.'

But the absent days were unlucky ones for both man and dog. A few miles down the valley a pack of stray dogs had attacked sheep in fenced inland fields, savaging several and leaving deadly open wounds in their sides and hindquarters. The brown dog was seen among them and positively identified.

'That dog would do no harm,' young, fiery-haired Paddy Rua asserted.

The accuser, a tall shepherd like Paddy himself, shook his head. 'You know yourself,' he said, 'it's the best dogs go to kill sheep the quickest.'

It was the fatal defect of the sheep dog. The gathering instinct that men put to work for themselves was descended from savage tactics of survival, from a time when all dogs lived only by their skill in hunting, gathering and killing. All sheep farmers knew that. It was common in their talk, and Paddy Rua could not deny the argument.

For a while he was silent. He looked about the farm kitchen at the faces of the old people sitting near the fire or at the bare wooden table. But they only turned to face the fire or rose and walked through the open door.

'All right,' Paddy said at last. 'The dog will be put down.'

When Brock came back the following morning Paddy Rua tied one end of a piece of brown grassrope around the dog's neck, from long practice and custom carefully knotting it in such a way that it could not slip or tighten on the animal's throat, and then tied the other end of the rope to a thin poplar that grew opposite the kitchen door. He climbed the hill to where he had left his gun behind the curtain of ivy leaves and brought it down with him to the house. As he approached, Brock, lying at the base of the tree, raised his head to watch in puzzlement. In the house Paddy Rua slowly removed all traces of the heavy grease he had smeared on and in the gun before leaving it under the rocks. Carefully he measured out a quantity of black powder and poured it into the gun's long single barrel, following it with a bit of wadding drawn from the shoulder of an old and ragged tweed jacket, ramming it firmly into place with a long willow rod. Then he added small grains of shot, and more wadding, and rammed again. The whole process of loading the gun took him almost a quarter of an hour. Satisfied at last, he took the gun and went out.

The dog was gone. A shred of chewed rope was all that remained trailing from the thin poplar.

Paddy Rua stood for a moment without moving, the long gun balanced in his right hand. Then, without thinking, he raised his eyes to the green slope that rose behind his thatch house, and watched the small brown form of the dog rising slowly upwards, rising and stopping to look back, as he had always done when working sheep, as though this time too he were looking back to the man for gestured instructions, not running impetuously but making his way by slow degrees up the steep hill-side. Paddy Rua stood below and watched the dog ascend until he had reached the spink. Slowly and carefully, as always in the past, the dog rose above the spink, walked along the top, returned down the far side, and walked out on to the narrow ledges, just as he had done so often when turning the trapped sheep out of them. Then he sat.

Paddy Rua started upwards, the loaded gun balanced easily in his hand. He followed the dog's own route, but stopped on the near side of the spink, parallel with the ledge on which the dog sat. Planting his feet firmly into the green sward at the edge of the spink and inclining his tall body slightly forward, he raised the gun to his shoulder. For a moment he looked along the barrel until it was steady in his grip, then he fired. The dog collapsed quietly on to the narrow ledge and lay still.

At that moment in his recollections Paddy Rua stopped. A definitive halt in his thoughts intervened. He had no desire to remember or recall any further. A trace of an old man's bitterness and resentment crossed his features. He took off his cap, momentarily revealing the fine white hair that covered his head, and then replaced it firmly with a twist.

'But the other dog were got, you see,' Mary interposed.

Paddy Rua looked into the fire again.

'Aye.'

He paused.

'It weren't many days after that, there were more sheep tore, and they got the dogs at it. And the brown one in it, it weren't Brock at all. Brock was dead in the spink.'

'It weren't Brock at all,' Mary echoed. 'And then they kilt the ones were doing the killing, but Brock was dead then.'

'Aye, Brock was dead,' Paddy Rua affirmed. He had ended his story, and he pushed himself up, gently, precariously, from his low stool by the hearth, and went to the wooden table in the corner of the kitchen.

But Mary, pouring tea from the old aluminum tea-pot into a plain white cup, went on.

'Weren't it funny, though, about the sheep after that?'

Slowly Paddy Rua began to eat the bread his wife had smeared with butter for him, softening it in his mouth with small sips of the hot tea. For him the story had ended.

But Briney Paddy Rua, returned from the hill, had heard his mother's last words, and resumed again.

'It were funny,' he began. 'But there's Brigid Phil across the river and old Jimmy Wee Jack, the next winter after, when the three yirrols came across the hill, driven ahead of the storm, and went into the spink, they were watching that time, and what was it put the yirrols out again?'

38

'Ones be saying different things,' Paddy Rua answered. 'You wouldn't know the half of what they be saying.'

A reluctance to remember more had come over him, and the story of the brown badger-like dog was at an end, but Mary, as though echoing her husband's last words, revived the smothered recollections.

'Aye,' she said slowly, pausing in her sweeping of the flagstones, 'one's be seeing different things. You wouldn't know at all what they be seeing.'

Paddy Rua's eyes glowed again with memory, and he raised his hand very slightly above his knee.

'I seen it me self,' he said, 'seen it often after that. And for years more, when the hard winter was in it, there was no sheep lost in the Black Spink, for the wee brown dog were in it still, Brock, to put them out again, a brown spot back and forth on the face of the spink, in snow and all, and the sheep turning and coming out again, quiet, slow, till they be safe.'

His raised hand moved in a small arc, a matter of inches, slowly back and forth above his knee, as though recalling, or trying to recall, the back and forth movement of the brown dog. Mary and Briney watched him and looked, as they seldom did, at his eyes, as though trying to see what he saw. Mary, like many others, had seen the sheep come out of the spink in the midst of heavy winter snow, and even in storms. Sometimes, watching, she thought she saw something moving near them, a small dark form putting them out of the spink. She could never be sure.

Word had slowly gone down the river and into the valley below that the Black Spink had lost its power to trap sheep. Sheep went in, but they came out again. Older men and women nodded quietly over the matter and recalled the history of Paddy Rua's loyal brown dog, wrongly accused, that he himself had shot in the very same spink. Younger men pointed out that rocks had fallen from the spink in a spring thaw and that the ledges had probably widened, allowing the sheep to turn and escape. But in the hills, the hill farmers themselves watched from time to time as sheep came out, and sometimes they followed Paddy Rua's intense look, knowing that he saw something in the spink, something that was working the sheep, turning them around, driving them out. Then they looked back to the spink, saw the sheep moving to safety, and tried to see

39

more. It was not certain that any succeeded.

It was certain, however, that the sheep could not have got out of the spink on their own. Every hill farmer knew that, and some had even seen the sheep move – as sheep never moved – into the driving winds and blowing snow.

'But sure,' Briney said, 'the sheep will always stand with their tails against the storm, never face into it.'

But the story was confused. There were some who said that sheep *were* lost in the spink and that it was only Paddy Rua's old ewes, ones that had been in the spink before and been driven out by the brown dog, and so in a manner trained to come out of it – that it was only those sheep that came out of the spink again. Everyone had a different idea of the truth.

Paddy Rua went back to the fire and sat on his low stool.

'There were no sheep lost in it for years,' he said. 'But then people was talking, saying all kinds of things. Damn, there were no harm in that brown dog that people should take alarm.'

'The priest come up,' Mary explained. 'People were after him to come, I suppose, and he come up to see.'

'Aye,' Paddy Rua resumed. 'The priest come up in his robes and all, a big crowd with him, a *precession*, and up the hill, and beyont, to that lough that's in the hills, and laid him to rest in that lough. That's the wee silvery lough has the trouts in it. Laid him to rest in that lough. That was years ago.'

Paddy Rua stood on his street again looking up towards the Black Spink.

'Right there, where you see that bit of white fleece. That's where a sheep went in last winter and never come out again. That's a bit of the wool. Right next to that, that's where the dog was kilt.' He stopped for a moment, looking towards the spink, and then added his final comment.

'Thon was a loyal dog,' he said.

Later, in the kitchen again, Paddy Rua remembered the gun that had killed the dog.

'Het was the last time ever I used it. I left it then back in the wee cave behind the ivy, and it was only later, after they laid the dog to rest, that I minded the gun, and went up to see about it. And it was there still, but the grease all away off it, and the barrel rusted out. It was rusted out, you see, like fine lace. You would say it was like fine lace. And when I went to lift it out the light went through it like the lace, and it went away then into little bits. Away into tiny bits. Away entirely.'

THE RUSH

The rush was the first thing I noticed. The rushes everywhere, through the meadows and grazing lands, clumps and broad areas of blemishes on the fine greenness of the land. 'That old blue till,' I was told, 'that old blue till can never be drained right.' That was the cause of the rush, the bluish-grey clay that impacted itself just below the fertile soil and resisted penetration of the surface water to deeper levels. It meant that the land was also a kind of solid lake, a constantly wet mass on which the weeds of wetness thrived. When the weather dried up the ground's condition grew worse. With no deeper level of moisture to draw on the usually soggy clay quickly hardened and cracked. Deprived of rain for a few days the grass ceased its growth. Only the rush retained its foothold and flourished.

So to me the rush appeared only as an ugly weed that was everywhere, and I learned to associate the dark stalk, with its little clump of seed pods on one side near the top, with the wet fields churned into mush by the sharp hooves of lean cattle. A huge part of the back of my own hill was covered in rushes so dense that it was difficult to push through them. I asked an old man, whose indeterminate date of birth was somewhere around the beginning of the century, how long they had been growing there. 'As long as I mind,' he told me.

It was all part of the general problem of weeds that preoccupied me constantly in the first years. Weeds grew everywhere, were abundant on what I learned to call my 'park', those few acres of fenced and green land that some earlier generation of farmers had reclaimed with lime and manure from the coarse heather of the hill to serve as meadow, to yield the mountain hay that was never ready to mow until August, never won until the wet and blustery final weeks of September, the cocks never carried in to be built into a stack until the short, anxious days of October. My eye saw no use in those weeds, saw only blemish. Later I would hear some of the old farmers talking of the worth of those weeds as fodder and questioning the merit of pasture that was limited only to grass itself. Oddly, I discovered, there was almost no weed that some farm animal would not graze. The broad leaves of dock that expanded with terrible rapidity into the after-grass that followed the first – my first – cutting of hay caught my attention and I found out that they were a 'notifiable' weed, by which was meant that it was an offence to have them on your land. By law every farmer was required to spray the dock that grew on his land and so poison it. I wondered if there was another way and was told they could only be dug out, but that the root went very deep and any bit left over would grow again into a full and strong plant. A legend told of the stranger who had appeared at a fair many decades before selling the seeds of a marvellous new plant. Gullible farmers had bought and tried the seed: from it had grown the first dock plants, never again to be eliminated from the green fields. I, fresh to farming, continued to look for a cure.

'Don't worry about them dockens,' an old farmer told me, his only literacy his memory of what he had heard from others or himself observed. 'When you put your cow out in the morning she'll grab a couple of them dockens, and she'll grab a couple more in the evening when you go to put her in, and there'll be a rich cream on the milk after them. October, this is the month for the dockens.'

I found it hard to believe. The dock was a weed, it could hardly enrich the cow's milk. It was, I thought, part of the mechanism of life in the poor hills, to value what you had, lest, despising it, your courage should collapse. Even the weeds were to be respected. But I watched the cow as I put her out and, strangely to me, saw her wrap her long, broad tongue around the first dock leaves she encountered in the morning, chewing them eagerly, then ignoring them until when, as I was told she would, she hastily snatched one or two more on the way home to byre and stall at night. Even odder, I thought, was that the milk did grow richer and creamier. I mentioned the episode to a more modern keeper of cattle on a farm nearer the sea. He listened with open mind. 'Now I never would have thought that,' he said finally. 'The dock is a notifiable weed. I always spray mine.' It was the first hint I had of the

43

discontinuity between hill and valley.

If the dock was a useful weed, was in fact fodder, there was no reason to hate it as I had. Digging my vegetable garden later and pondering as I did so the mysterious nature of earth and soil, I learned that the dock was indeed the most persistent of plants, that its thick, hard root penetrated and survived at a deeper level than any other, nourishing the broad leaves that shaded and smothered all growing things around. Noticing that its root was the only one that entered into and cracked the hard, rust-coloured layer of infertile clay that lay a foot or so below the surface of the ground, I speculated on the possibility that a phase of dock all across the farm would not be the worst thing for the land, that the heavy roots would open it up at a deeper level than any grass could do and so provide a drainage and a path for the roots of the grass itself.

But in the end I found that dock could be controlled by cutting it with a scythe two or three times a year, yielding each time with less resistance to the blade, until it almost disappeared. It was easy to believe that the rush would do so too. My land was full of weeds. I stood looking across the park in perplexity and admiration of their density. That first June when I came up to start the long task of remaking the shambles of house and farm in the wetness of almost steady rain I took solace in the chaos and loneliness of the hill from the sudden appearance one morning of yellow irises on the park. Taking my careful steps down the slippery grass of the slope, I got a closer look at a large oval patch of stiff sharp leaves in the shape of sword blades. In the middle of the patch a deep hole, and later I would realise that an old piped drain – piped with heavy natural flagstones – had collapsed at that point in its course. The three or four plants that had flowered that morning were what I noticed, rightly conjecturing that fresh cut flowers would reconcile my wife to a large extent to the hardships of our primitive living conditions then. The other flowers that filled the meadow after I had put the sheep off it performed the same task: tiny white daisies, miniature pink wild orchids, buttercups, deep blue hare-bells and others whose names we did not discover. Not far from the wild irises were several equally broad clumps of nettles. Someone passing by while I was looking at them informed me that a load of byre manure had been dumped there for spreading but never had been spread. I found out from my own experience later that thick forests of nettles always developed on unspread manure. One autumn I tried a donkey on the park, letting the sheep and cattle graze it down first and leaving the donkey with the job of cleaning up the remnants. He went to work on the thistles first. I noticed how delicately and carefully he took them into his mouth – was it his lips he was protecting? – and then chewed them up with obvious pleasure. He ignored the iris but went on to the nettles, chewing them into the ground and then pawing up the roots and pulling them out with his front teeth and chewing them up as well. I congratulated myself on this simple success without effort on my part, but in the spring, just when the weather was mending and the fresh grass beginning to grow, the donkey died – the victim of my foolishly transferring him too soon from gentle park to coarse hill grazing – and the nettles, far from defeated, came back with primitive freshness and strength. In the end I found that, like the dock, cutting the nettles and wild yellow irises two or three times in the course of a summer gradually weakened them and let the grass gain a grip around them.

But the rush was different. 'Cut them and you'll banish them,' I was assured, and on that assurance I wielded my scythe furiously, quixotically, against thousands of clumps of rushes. Disappointingly, the rushes always grew again. 'I mind the time,' a neighbour said, 'when you wouldn't find a rush growing anywhere around here for miles.' He paused for emphasis and I contemplated the white brush of hair that covered his head, much as the stiff clumps of rushes covered so many acres of the surrounding hill, and wondered how many years before he was thinking of. 'Man dear, men were going miles into the hills and carrying back burdens of rushes – a burden of rushes is far heavier nor a burden of corn, you know – to thatch the houses and the byres. You wouldn't get a rush near hand. If you wanted to thatch a stack of hay or one of turf itself you had to go way into the hills for the rushes.'

We discussed the matter for a while in similar terms, and then he assured me: 'That's the reason there are so many rushes about now. There's no one to cut them, you see.'

So the rush could not be banished, only cut, and cut again, over and over, always to return, a permanent guest on the land. Contemplating the image of men climbing far into the hills carrying scythes and stones for cutting the rushes and ropes for binding the cut and gathered rushes into the heavy burdens, then carrying all together the long journey back again, I realised that the rush had not always been unwanted. Adversary in my sense, it was also an ally, a useful weed that provided thatch over everything that was to be protected from the falling rain, and also bedding under animals to keep them from the damp clay floors of their stalls. I remember going to assist at some sheep work one day and admiring the thick clean bed of green rushes that had been prepared in the yard the sheep were to be put into, striking contrast to the muddy dishevelment of my own yard, where I had not yet learned the trick. Finally I heard one of the oldest of the local farmers – a tall, thin man in his eighties who never ceased to regret his declining ability to do his own farm work – say that he thought that a good field without rushes wasn't a good field at all.

'I wouldn't have it,' he said.

Was it the consolation of the poor farmer, then, on his poor land? There was the story of the blind man who wanted to buy a farm of good land for his son. 'Put me on my horse,' he said, and the son put him on the horse and then led him down the road. Whenever they came to a farm of land that was for sale the blind man would ask his son whether he saw any rushes. 'Yes,' the son said at last, after a number of rush-free farms had been left behind. 'Hitch my horse to a rush bush.' The son did. 'This is the farm,' the father concluded.

Fighting the weeds, I decided at first that it was indeed just that – the consolation of the poor farmer on poor land. Later, when I had lived the life myself for a while, I wondered. Rushes, I learned, were associated with well-limed land and fine friable soil. Where rushes were, good crops of oats and potatoes might also grow, or heavy meadows.

But on unfenced, abandoned land near mine I saw that the rushes had spread until they had become like a sea, a dense carpet of smothering stalks that blotted out the grass. And what about the score or more of acres of almost impenetrably thick rushes that grew on the back of my own hill?

'Wait until spring,' a near neighbour suggested, 'when the real drying comes, and the east wind. Man, the rushes will be as dry as tinder then. Set a match to them and be done with them, and the green grass will grow up after them then.' Another neighbour assured me that rushes never burned. To decide, I chose a small isolated clump of rushes near a lake, waited for the dry weather, set the match. A fierce yellow flame flew forth from the first clump and an intense heat, and then as the flame appeared to be dying out it communicated itself suddenly by way of the strands of dry brown grass at the base of the rush to the adjoining clump. As the fire climbed swiftly into the air again I felt the intense heat once more, though only for seconds, and as it was again dying away once more it travelled to the next clump, and so on through the eight or ten clumps of rushes, finally dying out for good.

I tried to imagine the burning of twenty acres of dry rush, imagined the intensity of the heat, wondered about a sudden wind, thought it wise to seek further counsel before striking the irrevocable spark. It was during a break while cutting turf for an old farmer not far from me. The dry weather – the 'winning weather' – had come, and it was time to get the turf cut and set out to dry. We had cut the first floor of a bank of turf not far from his house and were resting then, sitting on the dry heather and looking across over valley and river at the very rushes I had it in mind to burn, and at the new sheep-fence my neighbour and I had just put up between us to keep our flocks separate, its strands of still bright wire gleaming in the warm sun, the still freshly cut posts of larch on which the wire was stretched themselves reflecting the warm light.

'Oh aye,' my friend said. 'A good idea, too, to burn them rushes.'

He paused and stuffed his pipe with the morsels of tobacco he had cut and then milled between his rough palms.

'You would be done with them then. A good idea.'

He paused again as he struck a wooden match and drew the flame deeply into the briar bowl and over the dry crumbs of tobacco.

'It's a good way to be done with the rushes,' he concluded.

I took heart. He was, I knew, a man of much experience in the hills. With his approval I could safely go ahead. I began to visualise the twenty acres freed of rushes putting forth a soft grass manured by the ash itself.

'But what about the man that set a rush fire that time?' He glanced towards me and away again, drawing deeply on his pipe.

'That time, that was years ago. He had a mind to banish the rushes, you see, and he never told no one. Set the fire one morning and away.'

Again he paused and puffed.

'Wait, let me tell you,' he resumed. 'The fire banished all the rushes, every one. Not a rush left. And then it leapt on to the heather – do you have any heather on that hill? – the heather is very quick to burn, and it burnt all the heather. And then the bog itself took fire. It was that dry, the bog itself began to burn, and nothing to stop it. They were out then, man dear, the whole countryside was out with spades and shovels, and couldn't stop it. It burnt all before it then, stacks of turf from the year before, that had stood through the winter and no harm come on them, went away in flames, and fences' – he looked at my new fence and then at me – 'aye, fences were burnt into the ground, every larch stab, and the wire twisted and rusted after it and useless then. And it took a stack of hay with it, and only it stopped just in time it would take a byre with it next, and the house beside it. Aye!'

He looked squarely at me.

'And the one that set it, he was known. And they could have him for it, too, only they said, enough harm done – he ruined his own land, you see – let him go. But he never made no good after it. No. He never did. And he died soon after.'

With the perfect timing of the practised speaker, my friend dropped his discourse at that point and never mentioned it again through all the rest of the long day during which we cut and spread his bank of turf, and I myself put the matter from my mind. Later I went to look at the rushes I had burnt and found them growing again fresher and greener than before. So the burning had been a form of pruning, and pruning meant renewal. It was another of the standard themes of Donegal hill talk, the rejuvenating effect of pruning. I heard it said of fish in a lake or of foxes in a wood that was overrun with them, even of insects. The old farmer reasoned about nature and living things in interlocking chains of being from one thing to another, and when he wanted an animal to die out he left it alone, and when he wanted it to flourish he hunted it, fished it, culled it.

Was the same true of the rushes? Back home I knew I would resort first to poison, to destructive sprays and powders, noxious at times to the sprayers and dusters themselves in spite of their clumsy protective clothes and masks. Some farmers here, too, had tried the sprays, with oddly little success. Success, that is to say, for a year or two, until the deeply hidden remnants of root put forth new and even denser growth. The nature of the land had not been changed by the spray.

A younger farmer, miles away, near the shore, an avid hunter, talked of the culling of foxes. 'We shoot them out of the forestries one year, and they're better by far the next. But a few years back, when there was no shootin' in the plantings, they almost died out. Lice, mange, disease, you see, be to finish them nearly.'

I wondered if there was no way to eliminate the fox, enemy of lambs, and so of farming and farmers. Strychnine? To which he answered with the parable of the fox that got the strychnine, but when the body rotted a goose from a nearby farm was killed by the same bit of strychnine, and a dog that ate the goose died then. The strychnine never disintegrates, never deteriorates or returns to the land, he told me. Instead it remains, to kill and kill again.

What answer to all this then, I wondered?

'Nature,' he said. 'Nature. All things must live, and we will live among them. Leave the foxes alone. Nature will keep the balance.'

I followed the direction of his thinking then when I looked at the rushes, at the sea of rushes that choked broad acreages on the back of the hill. Leave them alone, let them flourish to the point of death. And what about the grass? Was not the grass an ally? And the heather? If the sheep that steadily cropped the grass and heather were kept from that stretch of hill for six months of the year, the six months when grass and heather grow best, would they, the grass and the heather, not fight the rush? Would they not drain the land with strengthened, ever deeper roots, sucking up more and more of the moisture, drying the land, pushing out the rush, robbing it of the wetness it could not live without? It was worth trying. But it was slow, a project of years, not one season, a long, slow, patient process, not as swift as poison, not as easy. It meant letting the living herbage strike its own balance, amend the condition of the land itself, in its own slow way. But it would be without poison, and it would be more lasting, until the next uncontrolled invasion of the sheep.

In time, slowly, I saw the change develop, year by year, the grass and the heather dry the land, extend their area bit by bit, invade the heart of the fading, withering rushes. Broad areas of rushes, where once neither I nor any sheep could walk, thinned out, weakened, failing, leaving the ground for the grass, until finally, when they had given ground enough, I too wondered whether I wanted them all entirely banished from my land. In heavy winter snows I saw the hungering sheep live for days on the green tips of the rushes and, as the snow receded, on the heavy grass trapped and dried at the root, a natural winter hay, a natural life-saving provision.

No wonder the poor farmer of the hill did not despise the rush, did not see it, as I saw it, as his enemy. For he saw nothing as his enemy, not rush, or dock, or thistle, or nettle, or any weed, and not the foxes either and the swarming rabbits that I so hated, but saw all things as part of an interlocking chain and cycle and harmony. It was, I saw at last, more than the consolation of the poor farmer. It was part of his understanding of the way things really are. The rush that thatched his house and byre and stacks of hay and corn and turf, that bedded his animals, and often foddered them in winter – it, too, was life. The symbol, possibly, of life, when, every first day of February, he wove it strandwise with his hands into a simple Brigid's cross and presented himself at his neighbour's door, and carried into the house the cross of fresh green rushes, chanting an old formula that he would never question: *sheh baha, sheh baha, sheh baha* – it is life, it is life, it is life.

THE EXTRA WETHER

A house, a home, a house-raising after a wedding. Strong men quarry irregular stone with crow-bar and pick from the hillside. With gravel and clay for mortar and fill they fit the rough, unshaped stones together into slowly rising walls. Brown peat-saturated tree trunks preserved in the deep bog, sleeping centuries there before this resurrection, rise rough-hewn to become roof beams and rafters, their parings laths. Grass sods, cut like carpets from the earth, cover them over, and then the heavy rushes mown with swinging scythes from the boggy slopes around complete the roof. The house has grown from the ground it stands on.

'That's it done now,' the builders comment. 'We weren't long at it.'

In the narrow stone kitchen a small window lets in a glimmer of light, the gleam falling on the hard-packed clay floor. A table folds on hinges up and away against the wall. A high sideboard with china bowls, cups, plates; two low wooden chairs, a bench, a stool; and the hearth, the centre of the life of the house, its fire glowing orange in the gloom around it.

A tall, slender man moves in with his short, slight wife, and the life of the house begins. A glowing turf brought in from the wife's home starts the new fire. The large and heavy, round-bellied cast iron pots, newly purchased in the town, are soon soot-blackened. Brigid sits on the low stool before the fire, folds her arms across her stomach, rocks back and forth and remembers her childhood.

'I was born in America,' she recalls. 'In Chicago.' She pauses to allow her hearer to absorb the information, then adds an affirmation of her words. 'Aye. I was.'

John, sitting on a wicker chair a yard further back from the hearth, laughs softly and comments, 'She be's a Yank.'

'And I weren't only four years old when I come home,'

Brigid continues, and remembers the deaths that were the earliest part of the memories of her beginning life. 'My father, he died over there, you see, and my mother bring us home.' And other deaths not remembered but recalled from her mother's talk. 'My brother, he weren't only two years, and my sister, she was four month.'

Her mind goes back to her own recollections, the earliest things she can still see in memory. 'I mind the horse leppin'. Isn't that funny? That's the first thing ever I mind. He must have took a scare.' Then, when she thinks, she remembers one thing before that, the lights of the port glowing red.

'But I mind nothing of America.'

Her thin body swells and from the swelling comes a boy. She swells again: a girl. The boy grows like his father, tall and slender, the girl like her mother, short and thin. As the four live and change, so does the house. A curtained bed is built into the corner of the kitchen beside the hearth, near the warmth, protected from stray draughts, darkened within for sleep. The house lives its own life, matures, ages. Thatch decays, stones shift. After the heavy work of the farm with cattle, sheep, turf, corn, hay, potatoes, comes the repairing – all hard work, labour enough for more than one strong man. The blackbird tears the thatch in her search for living food, a storm wind lifts a corner of the roof, the pouring rain seeps through the wall, dissolves the clay and shifts the stone. Then the work is urgent, skilled neighbours gather, and the cycle begins again.

In the three-room house the four live together amidst the natural world that surrounds them, infinitely neat in their perfect organisation of the small space of the house with beds, cupboards, shelves, the sleeping loft added as an afterthought, tables, chairs, benches, stools. The hearth, the focus of the living house, glows with a perpetual fire. Once ignited it has continued from itself without a break, kindled anew each morning from the glowing coal of turf hidden beneath the ash the night before. As the house decays and is repaired, the mortal life within declares in the hearth its will to survival.

Though Brigid had come home from America, for most farmers it was a time for leaving the hills and farms. Elsewhere there were jobs. For those who stayed there was the dole. Once a week each man went down to sign for the dole, once a year he presented his sheep for the government bounty. For them dole

52

and bounty were the best part of staying alive, but still the hills grew emptier, and the comment was often heard from those who remained, 'The hills will soon be waste.'

For young Condy and Hannah the prospect was of a long bachelorhood and a long spinsterhood stretching into old age and death. They would not be the first brother and sister to live out their lives in lonely shared solitude, seldom conversing, attuned to a slow routine of bowls of tea and plates of boiled potatoes, the brother spending days on the hill after sheep, the sister milking the cows, feeding the hens, tending the fire. They learned that routine even as children and started early to relieve their father and mother of the work. Brigid, still a girl, thinner even than her mother, leapt quickly to her feet when there was a task about the house, water to be fetched from the spring, hens to feed, eggs to collect, cows to milk. Condy went to the hill to look through the sheep and learned early in life to enjoy his long wanderings there without food, often in a drizzling mist, his daily visits to the haunts of the scattered ewes, sheep he knew and recognized easily, whose ways he learned. Returning late, he brought down a creel of turf for the fire. Then the tea, milk, bread and butter was put before him, or the steaming potatoes for his dinner. He sat at the wall-hinged table, his back to the others, and ate in silence, chewing thoughtfully, slowly. Mother and sister sat behind him, arms folded, watched him eat, jumped up to put more tea into his cup, slice more bread, put out more potatoes from the pot on the hearth. So used were they all to one another, to the farm's routine, its animals, its functionings, that communications had long ceased – if ever – to be sentences, or even phrases, and became instead words, syllables, looks which according to the time of day meant one thing or another, alluded to this or that simple ever-recurring task. An outsider, even a near neighbour perhaps, would scarcely understand these abbreviated, whispered references, given in private words and pet names, in movements of hand or head or body, to animals and tasks, a family dialect.

The family had heard itself out so many times that there was little more to say. Gossip became all-important, information picked up weekly on signing-day by the men, fortnightly on shopping-day by the women.

'Nothing strange?'

'Deal a much.'

But young Condy and Hannah still had reason enough to talk to each other. Their world, that had become so ordinary to their mother and father, was new to them still and they felt a private wonder at what they saw and lived. A little thing could be important.

What about the extra wether? Quinn, the jobber, had come to buy the wether-lambs. Twenty-two, herded into the yard between old stone byres and sheds the night before. The yard gates were the discarded ends of an old bedstead. John propped them securely shut with heavy poles, then stood looking over them at the gathered lambs.

'Ought to go a good price, them 'uns,' he commented. 'Them's good lambs.'

But Quinn took only sixteen of the twenty-two, leaving the six smallest.

'Put them small ones out,' he decided, 'and I'll give you one-eight-and-six for the remainder.'

Quinn, a short, compact man with orange hair and a bright, square freckled face, wore a neat grey suit. He backed his oversize horse-box up to the bedstead gate. Condy looked on and leaned forward, uncertain.

'Sure, we'll take them out by ones,' he said. 'Safest that way.'

Quinn vetoed Condy's suggestion. 'Not at all.' The jobber had a quicker method: grab hold of one wether by the horn and, emitting a loud soprano bleat in imitation of a lamb, drag it aboard the horse-box. The other lambs would follow on after the leader.

John was incredulous. 'Them's wild lambs. They'll scatter on you.' But Quinn was sure of his method, and a moment later men and dogs were out in wild and noisy pursuit of the fleeing wether-lambs. Loud confusion followed, as always when too many men and too many dogs tried to do the work best done by one man and one dog. Quinn sent out his dog with sharp, rapid commands, John sent out his, Condy sent out his, and the three dogs encouraged each other to fierce and terrifying barks, driving the lambs to frantic leaps and bounds scampering in disarray across the hills.

Getting them together was a chaotic gathering of sheep, some not gathered at all but rather captured as they threw themselves to the ground and froze in terror of the panic shouts

54

and barks. Condy felt the rapid pulsing heartbeat of the last one as he brought it in and heard Quinn declare crisply, 'That's it. Good man. Have them all now.'

But oddly, later in the year, when they came to gather the remaining six lambs, they had seven.

John smiled quietly. 'Could be we had twenty-three alway,' he commented in thick, amused tones. 'Might be we had no twenty-two at all. 'Twas twenty-three we had.' He paused and looked around again at the others with the same quiet smile. 'Say nothing to Quinn anyway. S'pose he would ask if he had one missing. He would ask.' Another moment's thought, and then, 'Indeed, the wether could go a good enough price in the spring, if he be living.'

The others nodded and echoed assent. 'Aye. That's it. If he be living,' Brigid remarked, and John added one further comment on his own words: 'Wethers do be soft of themself. Maybe some of them wouldn't stand the winter.'

Brigid rocked by the hearth. 'If the winter be a good one?' she suggested. She smiled a long arc of a smile beneath her large curving beak of nose. 'Could go a good enough price in the spring.'

'That's it just,' John re-echoed, 'if the winter be a good one. Could go a good enough price in the spring.'

But that particular wether was marked by fate and destined to evade them all. Instead of staying with the rest of the flock he wandered miles away into the high hills above the farm. When Condy made the long plodding trip into the hills to get him, it took his and his dog's best efforts to block the wether's wild evasive actions and herd him back to the farm. The family began to call him 'the wild one'.

'What about the wild one on the back?' John would ask.

In fact he did become like a wild animal, running ever further into the hills at the sight of man or dog, getting himself on a high knoll squarely between Condy and the low winter sun, invisible in the overpowering glare but sending a shrill whistle of alarm through his nostrils. The time and effort needed to bring him in grew continually until at last he was left alone to pursue his ungregarious individualist life in the sparsely grazed hills, unbothered.

But one day another farmer stopped by the house to say that the wether needed attention. Maybe he had spent too much time on shaded north-facing slopes, maybe he needed a 'change of grass', or possibly just a dose of fluke and worm remedy. In any event, he clearly had taken 'the back-goin'.'

Oddly, it was in early spring, just when the fresh green grass was sprouting out of the ground, that sheep would fail. Having stood the rigours of winter snow and wind they weakened when milder weather and more abundant fodder came their way. But when Condy went out for the wild wether, to bring him down closer to the house, where he could be dosed and watched and put on the fields of 'kindly' grass, the wether, weak as he was and unable to flee even further into the hills, lay down and obstinately refused to walk on ahead of man and dog. The only thing to do was to bring the fluke and worm medicine out to the hills and dose him there, and hope that he would mend after the dose.

But luck was against the animal. Through the course of a severe winter he had grown a heavy fleece of wool that sprang thick and abundant from his back and flowed like a rich garment in long and silky strands to the ground. It was the weight of his own fleece that defeated him. As it grew heavier he grew lighter. Then one day he tumbled into a small hollow in the rough, heathery ground. Normally he would have righted himself with a kick of his legs and a twist of his body, but with the heavy fleece weighing him down the slightness of the hollow he had fallen into was enough to hold him trapped. He lay on his side, kicking futilely, one side of his body and head up towards the bright spring sky, the other pressed into the dark bog.

It was thus that the grey crow found him. Wheeling in broad arcs and descending spirals that covered square miles in matters of minutes, combing the ground with keen vision for possible helpless prey, the crow spotted the fallen wether. His cry of excitement reverberated from his high wheeling flight down to the slope below and sounded like the clinking together of two tiny hollow bottles. To any man or animal familiar with the sound it suggested ominous menace. The wether, hearing it, kicked still more fiercely but only became more securely stuck in the low hollow.

When Condy came over the crest of the hill he saw the wether at once. The brilliant white fleece, all the whiter for a winter in the pure air and clean rain of the hills, flashed out from where he had tumbled. Condy could not tell at first if the animal was still alive, or how long he had been in that position. As he approached he saw that it was alive and quickly he drew it up and stood it on its feet. The wether settled weakly to the ground and turned its head back so that one side of its face rested against its flank, the instinctive posture of the injured animal. From the other side of its head, the side open to the sky, the blood had gushed from the empty socket where the grey crow had pecked out the eye. The brilliant blood of the still fresh wound flowed opaquely red over the short black wool of the wether's face. It stood out in Condy's perceptions as the only spot of bright colour in the broad northern hill landscape of dull browns and pale greens, misty distant hills and grey sky. The intensity of the colour brought to his mind the association of blood and life, though he fashioned no words for the thought.

He plodded the long route home, got out the largest creel in the house, the one that took the biggest load of turf down from the bog, tested the ropes for soundness and strength, and then plodded back to where he had left the wether. Loading him carefully into the creel, he raised the load to his back and turned for home again, his arms crossed in front of him in visual token of the inner patience he would have to exercise to make the long carry down out of the hills and home.

Grazing the soft grass around the house, the wether improved and seemed destined for life. But the call of the hills to something wild in the animal was too strong. When a few weeks had passed and his strength began to return he wandered off again. This time Condy did not go after him.

'Let him go then,' John commented. 'He may take his chances.'

The chances were negative. After the warmth of March, April came in a month of fierce storms and high winds, and finally a heavy fall of snow. The snow lay on the ground for only a day or two, but there was enough to do with animals near the house without going to the hills for one wild stray. When the thaw came and spring began again Condy thought of the wether. As he reached the hills he saw at once from a distance the static white fleece brilliant against the still, quiet colours of the hill where grass had scarcely started to grow. The fleece, in flattened disarray against the dull browns and greens told, even at a distance, that the wether had died.

'Never were meant to have that 'un, s'pose,' John said, when Condy had returned.

'Aye, it does be hard to keep them all,' Brigid agreed.

'That's it. There's none as has them but loses them. Hard to keep them all.'

The only real conversation about the wether and its death was between young Condy and his sister. To their father and mother it was a matter-of-fact occurrence, something that had recurred so often in the past as hardly to be worth mentioning. A loss was best forgotten. Some men thought it a way of 'taking off the evil hour.'

But Condy told Hannah about his surprise – shock, almost – when he had first taken hold of the wether on the hill to feel what he thought at first was a huge growth on the animal's back, like a high, hard knob. Then, running his hand along it, he realized that it was the wether's own backbone. The animal had lost so much flesh that its bones stood out hard and high like marble knobs under the skin and fleece. But it was the fleece that deceived him. Over that skeleton without flesh the white wool had sprung thick and long, giving an appearance of well-being. In his independence on the north-facing slope of hill, under his full white fleece, the wether had been failing steadily throughout the winter.

Hannah, herself so thin, thinner even than her mother, the thinnest of any girl in those parts, sat by the hearth and thought of the dying wether. When she was alone she reached her hand carefully around to her own backbone to discover how much of it stuck out through her skin. In unconscious imitation of her mother she folded her arms across her chest and rocked back and forth before the fire.

Was there a plan, she wondered, for all animals and all people, that came with them when they were born, and stayed with them all their lives until they died: life for some, death for others, some married, some never, some to have weans, some none? Thinking about it, she concluded that some were for life, some not. The wether, she saw, was not meant to live. But when they were all together around the fire and the wether was mentioned, her only comment was an echo of her mother's words, 'It does be hard to keep them all.'

SACRAMENT OF THE SICK

Father Sean Ryan stood on the tarred street in front of the car showroom, idly watching the passing traffic, and speculating as he did so on the changes that were occurring in this small western corner of Donegal. His impression when he first arrived had been of the apparent stability of the region, so sharply in contrast to the English midlands where he had spent years as a city missionary. Donegal had seemed to him not merely stable but, in a sense, almost backwards. Long-established customs yielded slowly there and people were content with their own ways, their own lives, that seemed so simple to him. But now – the thought was reinforced by the volume of traffic on the road – he could see that west Donegal was in a state of transition. The old ways were proving inadequate and were, slowly still and gradually but inevitably, yielding to modern ones. Animal and man power was giving way to machine force. The horse was yielding to the tractor, the spade to the digger. The pony and trap was disappearing in favour of the car. In time the process of change was speeded up by a slight but definite money prosperity that was affecting the entire Western world, and with it Ireland. This modern prosperity had taken a long time to reach Ireland, and the last part it penetrated to was the extreme north-western corner of the island, but when it arrived at last, like a great wave that had travelled many miles and had spent all but its final force, keeping only the last faint ripples, it arrived slowly and steadily. It did not come in spurts and cycles, rising and falling, washing in at one moment and out the next. Slow, it was also steady. Steady, it was reliable. In arriving at last in Donegal, it had taken on the character of Donegal itself.

Yet it had also subtly changed that character. The new car dealerships that had sprung up in those years were one example, the improvement of the roads themselves another.

Main roads, like the one before him, had been widened and paved with a smoother surface, and the many untarred gravel tracks that led into the hills, rutted with rain and the rough gravel fill used in their construction, were yielding progressively to tarred surfaces. The tar itself was often irregular enough, of course, especially after a few seasons had passed and the grass and rushes of the old dirt track, more persistent than man's indifferent efforts to cover them over, had pushed through the new surface, and the over-full tractor-drawn loads of turf from the surrounding bog had sunk into soft places here and there, leaving hard to remedy cracks which were then exploited by the winter frosts. But even the cracked tar was better, from the motorist's point of view, than the old unpaved tracks.

When he had arrived in Donegal to take up, on a temporary basis, the position of priest at the Carrigmore chapel, Father Ryan was driving a small five-year-old Ford he had brought with him from England. Tipperary born, an Irish farm boy himself, he had never in his twenty years since ordination had a post in Ireland. Twelve years as a rural missionary in Korea had been followed by eight as a city priest in the slums of Birmingham. They had been years of service and were rewarding, but not in terms of money, and the old Ford, with its sluggish engine and lazy handling, was all he could afford in the way of a car. Its faults had been less apparent on the broad and even English roads than they were to become on the uneven terrain and long hill lanes of Donegal, and he soon learned that the Ford was no longer satisfactory. It was in fact too old to meet the demands of his new job. The problem of finding the money for a new one puzzled him for a while, but then it turned out to be easier than he feared it would be. In rural Donegal he was really not far in spirit from his home ground in Tipperary. Irish farming communities had much in common. Though in Tipperary they farmed cattle and tilled their land for wheat, while here in Donegal they kept sheep and few cattle, and their only crops were a patch of potatoes and a field of oats for home use, the minds of the people were much the same. One could be judged from the other, the unknown from the known.

He mentioned his difficulties with the car a few times in conversation to some of his more active parishioners, men in their forties and fifties who themselves had been driving cars or vans for ten or fifteen years. He brought it up when their wives had finished serving the tea and slices of home-baked bread and butter and had themselves sat down to listen to the talk. The community became aware of the single immediate problem facing their young priest – for to them, as a man in his early forties he seemed quite young, and something in his face and bearing also encouraged that impression. Once aware of his need they set about meeting it. Little discussion was required. A benefit would be held at the hall, the community centre, the long plain rectangular building of cement blocks, whose inner walls sweated a continuous layer of moisture throughout the year and whose wooden floors had warped and been adjusted more than once, but which had succeeded in its purpose of sharpening the social awareness of the community. A dance for the benefit of Father Ryan was announced, and held one Sunday night. Old and young were expected to attend, and apart from the entrance fee a certain number of spontaneous contributions were made at the door by those who were able to give. The satisfaction of the organizers was easily read in the door-keeper's attitude.

At first Father Ryan considered going to Dublin for his new car, where he would have a wider choice. Then he had decided to buy from one of the local men. The new dealerships had increased the range of possibilities available to him right in county Donegal itself, and he was able to shop around from one to the other looking for the best bargain. He had also heard good things about the newly introduced foreign cars, with their greater liveliness, and he decided to try one. He found one not much larger than the Ford, at a suitable price. The car, bright orange in colour, turned out to be a good one. Its only fault was a slackness in the brakes. Otherwise it was comfortable and easy to drive. Servicing and minor repairs were prompt. The Carrigmore community enjoyed seeing their priest in his new car.

From then on his financial condition had improved steadily. His appointment had been changed from temporary to permanent. The house he lived in was tied to the chapel and saved him the former burden of rent. His parishioners were generous, and they enjoyed the idea of holding an annual benefit for the priest they liked so well. He soon found that he had some extra money, as well as plenty of spare time, in this hardy community where not only deaths but marriages and births as well were rare. He talked to some of the members of the local gun club, who met every Sunday to shoot out the foxes that had multiplied in the Forestry Commission plantings in recent years, and bought a Spanish shotgun. The gun had been all right at first but then proved less equal to his demands as his boyhood skill in shooting, developed on an old but finely made English lever-action gun of the last century, returned. He traded in the Spanish gun for one made in Czechoslovakia, its fine dark steel barrels and delicately worked wooden stock themselves a visual assurance of the easy balance and precision of the gun's action. Soon it was known among the members of the club that when the priest fired at a fox the fox would fall.

Since he had free time during the week he acquired a terrier, and drove into the hills with his gun and his dog and sought out foxes and badgers there. Rabbits swarmed but they were easy game. The dog started an occasional hare and the priest usually bagged it, presenting it later to some parishioner whose taste ran that way. Now and then he came on snipe or woodcock and tested his skill, with increasing success, against them. These long rambles in the hills alone with dog and gun were a time of particular contentment for him. In contrast to his first two appointments, those of his missionary years, that had taken him to foreign countries and placed him among foreign people with foreign ways of thought, he was now among his own people again, people of his own race and nature and his own farming background. He liked them and they liked him. His bishop was also satisfied with him, and so he felt it possible that he had reached the stable resting-place of his final appointment. At the same time he was still young and vigorous enough to enjoy the strenuous hill walking, the exhilaration of the sport, even the challenge of the odd unexpected heavy downpour sweeping across the bare slopes and catching him away from shelter. He felt the muscles and sinews built up in youth on his father's farm, scarcely used now for so many city years, respond anew to the demands he made on them.

There was free time at night as well, for the parish provided him with a housekeeper who also did his shopping and cooking. The annual amateur theatrical, acted by the young people of the parish but directed by the priest, took up the slack of that free time for several winter months, as did occasional community functions during the rest of the year, but generally he preferred to stay away from community meetings. He felt that secular matters were not his proper business, meddling in such decisions could weaken his spiritual authority, and he noticed as well that his presence had an inhibiting effect on others there, making them less willing to speak out on the issues being discussed. So he avoided such meetings.

That summer he decided to take advantage of the newly opened Murvagh golf course, said to be the longest in Europe, and bought a set of golf clubs. On warm and sunny days, rare in Donegal even in summer, he sometimes drove down to the ocean for sunning and a swim. His parishioners, working their farms on such fine days, saw him pass by in his orange car. They liked having a lively, active priest who enjoyed life even while he took his responsibilities seriously. They liked the corresponding crispness of his sermons, his briskness at mass, the fact that he did not unnecessarily draw out the length of a funeral service. Father Ryan became a focus to the community.

When he had had the orange car for eighteen months he decided to trade it in for a new one. It had performed well, but there was no reason for waiting until it gave trouble. He chose a green one of the same model instead, and found it improved. The brakes, at least, were firmer. Eighteen months later the green one went for a blue one. In another year, however, the oil crisis and the rising price of fuel became a factor and he decided to try one of the new compact models. He kept that for a year too, satisfied with its low fuel consumption, but feeling increasingly cramped in its smaller space. Just at the time he had bought it a fellow priest had died, and Father Ryan had been asked to take over those parish duties in addition to his own. The new parish more than doubled his work. Being between the hills and the sea it was more densely settled and had more parishioners. There were far more young people among them and so there were also more marriages and baptisms. At the same time the work of his own parish had increased, for the ancient trend of emigration had reversed itself and young people were not only finding jobs to keep them settled where they had been born, but others who had left for work in England or Scotland were returning to Donegal, lured back by the quieter, more stable life of their own country, a better environment for raising their families than in the increasing violence of the cities, and also by the slow but even prosperity, a contrast now to the uncertain British economy. From having had too much free time the priest suddenly found he had almost no free time at all. His gun stood unused, his long ramblings in the hills a thing of the past, along with the pleasant hours on the golf links. His housekeeper, aware of the extra work he now had, made an effort to ensure that his meals kept pace with his burdens. His experience with a very small car in those circumstances convinced him that he needed a larger one again.

He had signed the papers trading over the one-year-old small car for the new bigger one (the transfer of the insurance from one to the other had already been arranged), and was standing on the tarred drive before the garage debating within himself whether to go into the garage to watch the mechanics giving the new car its final check and servicing before delivery, or to sit in the warmth of the small office, where the young woman receptionist was typing at her desk. It was a late January day and cold, but not extremely so. Snow had fallen on the hills a few days earlier and white ribbons of it had run part of the way into the valleys that descended southwards towards the sea, but then a thaw had followed and only remnants of the snow remained on the farms furthest into the hills, and like a mantle along the crests of the hills themselves. Blue Stack alone was still completely covered, a low perfectly moulded white dome. The day itself was indeterminate, neither overcast nor clear, but with long folds of pale orange light streaking the dull grey of the cloud cover from horizon to horizon. Though there had been no rain the roads and fields were wet. The air was neither warm nor cold. Too warm for January perhaps, and yet not comfortable.

He had just decided in favour of the office when the receptionist herself came out. He turned his eyes in her direction as she came towards him, expecting a polite suggestion that he should come in out of the cold. Instead, the receptionist told him that there was a phone call for him. Following her back into the office, he concentrated his energies, for he knew that he was now on duty. The call, to reach him at the garage, could only be an urgent one concerning one of his parishioners. Picking up the phone, he greeted his housekeeper without having to hear her voice first to know who it was.

'What is it, Bridie?' he asked.

'It's Rosheen Hannah, Father.'

'They want me?' he asked, by way of confirmation.

'Aye, Father. Her nephew is here. He says she's very bad. The doctor has been called as well.'

'All right. Tell him I'm coming now. They'll have the car ready for me this minute.'

'You know the way to the farm, Father? Have you been there before?' the housekeeper asked quickly, knowing that though Father Ryan had hunted all the hills and knew his way around them he seldom went into any of the houses, for he sensed the danger of embarrassing their occupants by a priest's unannounced visit.

Briefly they discussed the way to the high hill farm where the old lady was lying near death, the housekeeper sketching out the route by reference to the names of farmers whose land lay alongside the road. It was only when she came to 'the gate beside the road' and the lane beyond it that the priest was confused for an instant. He had pictured himself driving to the door of the house, as always. Now he was suddenly reminded that the house he was being called to was the one house in the region that had somehow remained isolated from the road and which could be reached only on foot. He had known of that circumstance but had never thought about it. He had never been to the house before.

Putting down the phone, he went out on to the street full of new and used vehicles to look for a sign of his own new car, reflecting on the irony that this first call he would be making in it would be to a house it could not reach. His mind's eye saw and travelled the gradually narrowing, gradually deteriorating asphalt track that climbed unevenly into the hills, coming at last to the point at Gallagher's lane after which the asphalt ended abruptly, giving way to a rude track of stone, gravel and mud, pocked with holes and wheel track ruts that left the centre awkwardly high for a modern car.

When, only twenty minutes later, he actually reached that place in the road, he piloted cautiously over it, mindful of the newness of the car, aware that he was still measuring the time of his ownership in minutes, not yet even in hours. The old road descended and curved, wide enough for just one vehicle at a time. After several hundred yards he reached a place where an old thatched house, its failing but still intact condition showing that it had been lived in to within a few years earlier, stood squarely in the middle of the road, or where the road, which turned sharply right and left to go around the house, hugging it as it went, should have been. After the house the road ascended again. He reached the gate beside the road that his housekeeper had told him about, a composite of old slabs and scraps of wood nailed together roughly, barely wide enough for a cow to pass through. He stopped the car and let his eye follow the lane that led through sloping meadow ground, bare then of grass, grazed clean as it had been by winter's hungry flocks, downward past a single-file stand of spruce to a hill stream and onward then to Hannah's farm and house. Having thus visually surveyed the path, his eyes automatically went to the sky. As he was facing north, he no longer saw the pale orange streaks cast on the low flat clouds by the otherwise invisible winter sun, but only the flat grey mist that normally hung about the crests of the hills in winter. He thought it would be wise to push on to where the street was wide enough for him both to turn and leave his car, and come back from there on foot.

As he drove the last few hundred cautious yards his mind returned briefly to his years as a missionary in Korea. He had often thought to himself, once he had learned some of the language and something about the ways of the people themselves, that the rural people of Korea were much like the rural people of Ireland in their ways of thought – preoccupations and concerns, calculations, plans – that a city man could not easily grasp, but which he, an Irish farm boy, more readily comprehended. He thought that, but did not express the thought to the other young priest, a native of Chicago, city born and bred, with whom he shared his duties, and who often stubbed his toe against unforeseen, to him at least, obstacles of custom or tradition. Sean, as fresh to Korea as his comrade, knew as little of the country and its ways as he did, but he also knew enough to feel his way cautiously through unfamiliar situations, to search for unseen pitfalls.

What took his mind back to Korea now was just such another summons, like today's, to deliver the sacrament of the sick to a dying peasant woman. The circumstances on that occasion were the exact contrary to those now. It had been the middle of summer, and as the warm morning sun progressed higher into the clear sky he navigated his motor scooter along ninety minutes of dry dust roads to a point where the road ended and he would take a ferry across a river, then ride another fifteen or twenty minutes to the small hamlet he had been summoned to. Arrived at the ferry wharf, he learned that he would have to wait in the increasingly hot sun for some half hour or more for the ferry's return. In all, the first half of his day's excursion took him over two and a half hours. At length he located the dying woman's house, and drove the scooter down a long and narrow lane – which, though level and dry and hence totally opposite to the moist hill path he had just surveyed, was nonetheless brought to his mind by it, the two moving side by side through their respective disparate landscapes like parallel threads in the woven texture of his experience – to the low wooden house. Seated on the floor of the porch, their legs straight out before them, their sandalled feet facing outward, were six or seven middle-aged or ageing peasant women. He was momentarily surprised that they had not risen and come forward to meet him, and wondered if he had arrived too late or if, more likely from their calmness, the dying woman was out of danger after all. Or had he come to the wrong house?

He composed his thoughts to muster his clearest Korean, and asked for the dying woman. There was a silence and a slight stirring but no reply.

'Where is the woman who is waiting to be anointed?' he asked, modifying the question.

Again the women stirred. Then one of them, apparently – as nearly as he could judge from his relatively short experience among orientals – not older than forty, leaned forward and said: 'It is I, Father.'

He looked at her, examined her features and studied her eyes.

'But you are not ill,' he said. 'Did you call me here to give you extreme unction?'

Again she paused, hesitating before her reply. The other

women looked on silently.

'No, Father, I am not ill, but I am about to go on a long journey, to a distant part of Korea, and I am afraid there will not be a priest there. In case of need I will not be able to receive extreme unction. Or if a priest is found, he will come too late.'

The young priest unbuckled the chin strap of his fine white summer-weight helmet and thought of the two hours of dusty road he had just travelled on his scooter, of the wait for the ferry in the hot sun, and thought of the equally long return journey ahead of him, all accomplished for nothing, over a peasant woman's misunderstanding of one of the sacraments of the Church. He explained, slowly and clearly, that he could not give her extreme unction if she were not actually dying. They discussed the matter, learned priest and ignorant peasant. In the end he had given in. He knew it was against Church doctrine to do so, but she had somehow persuaded him. Was it the thought that otherwise the day's long and uncomfortable travelling would be for nothing? Or was it her simple peasant guile? Or his feeling of sympathy with her, because of his own farm background? Or simply compassion? Perhaps he felt she was not entirely in the wrong in wanting this assurance of spiritual safety. Now as he drove the last few yards along the gravel road he reflected that in time, as it had turned out, the Church itself had modified its position.

He left the car in the farm street, bending his torso briefly over the half door and putting his head and shoulders into the kitchen long enough to greet the woman of the house.

'Hello, Sarah,' he said softly. 'How are you? I'm on my way over there now.'

'How are you, Father?' Sarah replied, coming to the door. 'They're waiting on you.' She looked across the narrow valley at the thatched house. 'It's chilly the day,' she added. 'You'll be wanting tea when you get back. I'll have it ready for you.'

He set off on foot down the unpaved road to the narrow gate. His mind went from its recent thoughts of Korea and the healthy peasant woman there to the one he was on his way to anoint, and whom he knew as a certainty was really dying. Knew as a certainty, because he also knew that priests and doctors were not summoned to these hills for any other reason. Unlike the other woman, unknown to him until she had spoken out on the porch, this one had been known to him as long as he had been in Carrigmore, known, at any rate, by sight, for he had never heard her voice. He knew of her only that for some fifty years, the greater part of a long life, she had been totally deaf, cut off by her deafness as well from virtually all converse with the rest of the world. To be deaf and also illiterate, he knew, was to be isolated from all the events of the great world that did not impinge directly – visibly or tangibly – on your own world. In the course of her long remoteness from the life developing around her and from the ever-progressing younger world, she had come to be thought of as wandering in her mind. The priest accepted that conclusion only with scepticism, but could say nothing for or against without talking to the woman herself, and she had never come to him. He had heard that she set out early every Sunday morning to walk the four miles down the hill from house to chapel, and then after mass he had noticed her slipping off wordlessly from the crowd for the return trip. By the time of his arrival in Donegal her walk had become a rapid hobble, as one leg grew increasingly lame. Sometimes, it was said, she became confused, mistook the day and dressed in her best clothes and embarked on the long walk on a weekday, refusing to be deterred or dissuaded from her purpose by those who met her on the way until she had actually reached the chapel and found it closed.

He had come to the gate. He saw that it was held closed by an old twist of cloth that served instead of a latch. It opened awkwardly. Going through and closing it again after him, he descended the lane that led to the stream below. As his foot slipped on the moist stones and grass he became aware of the inadequacy of his light shoes, their thin, smooth leather soles offering no grip on the sloping ground. The closely cropped meadow on either side of the lane, its low grass faded to a greenish yellow, appeared even barer from close up. Another gate, also pieced together of spare bits of wood, separated land from bridge.

He paused at the bridge of rough hewn planks without railings to inspect it for slipperiness. Beneath him the mountain stream, made fuller by the recent thaw, curled its way around grey rocks in a froth made tan rather than white by the fine particles of bog it carried with it from the deep turf of the hills. A small cascade just below the bridge, where the level of the stream dropped several feet from one set of rocks to another, sent up a thin, chilly spray.

Once across the bridge he quickly encountered another gate, this time nothing more than a short length of sheep fence stretched between two posts. He saw that opening it would be complicated and take time, so decided to climb over the fence instead, quickly locating the place where a slight rise served as a stile. Across the fence, his eye fell on a panel of thin aluminum that had been put there to close an awkward gap in the uneven ground below the lowest strand of wire of the fence. He recognized it at once, from the many similar panels he had seen near the gates of other hill farms, as a remnant of the airplane that had crashed high on Blue Stack one day of dense mist during the war. It was a reminder to him of another death, or deaths.

As he climbed the long steep meadow that was all that separated him now from the white stone house, still several hundred yards from him, he thought for an instant of his own farm days, when foot travel was his normal form of transport. As a young man of seventeen he had done all the ploughing of the farm behind a team of heavy horses, and herded cattle to and from the fairs. His free time was often spent hunting. Uneven ground, long treks, inclement weather, all had no effect on him, for he had been bred to them and had known no other land or climate than his native one. Now as his shoes slipped and grew moist on the wet ground he realized that much even of the condition gained in his not long abandoned hill rambles had left him. He was aware of breathing more heavily as he faced into the hill. His legs were labouring instead of responding effortlessly. He bent his head. As he did so he caught the faint thought within himself that, in spite of the discomfort he was feeling, it was somehow good to be on foot again, to feel the ground as he moved across it, through it: contact with earth.

The hill above the farm seemed higher now for his nearness to it and so intensified the sensation of the steepness of the meadow itself. Tattered rags of snow lay about its dull brown and grey surface, almost indistinguishable from the grazing sheep. A few sheep were grazing the inland slopes as well, and when he was about half way to the house he saw one of them coming towards him. He knew that it must be a ram, otherwise it would avoid the intruder to the farm, and its thick double-curved horns and heavy gait confirmed that guess. He felt a momentary flash of fear. Though he had handled steers and bulls often in his youth, their long, heavy horns no serious threat to him because he was used to their ways and he knew how to approach them, sheep were unfamiliar to him. He knew that rams could be dangerous, could back off to well beyond a man's arm's reach and then butt forward with the sudden speed and strength of powerful hind legs and the forceful impact of heavy skull and horns. He stood still watching the approaching animal, which stopped every few feet to raise its head and crinkle its snout towards him searchingly. In another moment he heard a voice calling from the house and a loud whistle. He saw a man in front of the house and the swift lope of a dog. At that moment the ram moved quickly off and away, as the dog came near.

'Come ahead!' he heard. 'There's no harm in that ram. He won't touch you.' It was the dying woman's brother, John. Awaiting the arrival of both priest and doctor, he had glanced out of the window and seen the impending confrontation of the ram and Father Ryan. Himself in his seventies, he was far younger than his dying sister and still vigorous. He greeted the priest warmly with his large, strong handshake, an accompanying smile on his face. Father Ryan, feeling the increasing inadequacy of his own shoes, looked involuntarily at John's heavy leather boots, then noticed that in every other respect he was relatively lightly dressed. The contrast between his own way of dressing, light shoes and heavy top coat, and the farmer's heavy footwear and flannel shirt and pullover, impressed him. The cold, damp wind that blew from the west penetrated his own coat but had no apparent effect on John, whose bright pink features and clear eyes showed his long adjustment to low temperatures and hardy conditions.

John led the way to the low thatched house, its unplastered stones newly whitewashed and strangely bright in the early twilight of the winter day which, though only beginning, had already begun to be felt on the hills. He instructed him to be cautious on the slippery flagstones of the drain that led away from the kitchen door, and warned him to duck his head for the low lintel. The interior walls were replicas of the exterior ones, rough, unplastered stone similarly whitewashed, the lime in its

71

many applications having softened and harmonized the contours and surfaces so that the uneven pattern of soft rounded grey-blue shadow and dull yellow light took on a kind of regularity to the eye. The warm light on the stones made him glance involuntarily towards the hearth, where a pile of turf had reached the state of a single fiery mass casting its warmth into the kitchen. Two plain wooden tables, one on either long wall, and a number of straight wooden chairs were all the furniture of the kitchen he saw. In a square niche beside the hearth he noticed a large alarm clock. As he caught sight of it he knew at once that it was not running. In a corner a young dog was tied to an iron staple that had been pounded into the wall. Two other dogs stood in the middle of the floor observing him curiously.

At either end of the kitchen a door led into an adjoining room, the house being built not in a cluster of rooms but in a train, a sequence. Father Ryan went into the room John pointed to. He was not surprised at the slightness of the dying form beneath the bedclothes, for he knew from many such visits how age diminishes the body, and approaching death, but what did surprise him was to see the old head turn at once in his direction as he entered. In view of her deafness he had not expected her to stir. Now he saw that she was fully conscious and even appeared alert, the colour had not entirely left her face, and her pale grey-blue eyes were still clear. A movement of the bedclothes told him that she was trying to bring her right hand out from under the covers to greet him in the normal way. The effort was abandoned in the lassitude of weakness. Instead, as he bent over towards her, so that she could see his face clearly, she spoke the only word he had ever heard from her.

'Father,' she said, the sound accompanied by a sudden rush of whispered air.

After the sacrament he refused both the offered cup of tea and the proffered glass of whiskey. John went with him to the first gate on the way down the slope towards the stream, forty or fifty yards from the house. As they walked, the priest cautiously watching his footing on the wet grass, John talked of the dying woman. She had been failing for some time. He had seen that she was not eating, but his efforts to coax her did no good. About ten days earlier, on a day of 'wild storm', she had put on her best clothes and set out for the chapel. He had seen that there was no good in trying to discourage her, so let her go, thinking she would soon turn back. Watching from the kitchen window, he had seen that when she was near the bridge across the stream the wind had blown her over and she had lain where she fell. He had gone down – 'it was a wild storm, you know, Father. It would test yourself' – and carried her back up to the house. From that moment she had not risen from her bed.

Half way down the long path through the meadow the priest stopped without thinking and turned back for another look at the fields, the house, the hills. His feet were wet through by then and the cold breeze felt even more penetrating than before, but he stood for a moment, looking. The thought he had had on the way over recurred now. There was something good about being on foot, in spite of the discomfort.

At the narrow bridge he met Sarah and the doctor. He saw at once that the doctor had never been to the dying woman's house before, but Sarah explained that to him nonetheless.

'I'll have tea for you directly I'm back, Father,' she added. 'I won't be long.'

'Don't hurry yourself for me, Sarah,' he said, not finding it necessary to add that he wouldn't want tea, remembering the warm meal his housekeeper had waiting for him back at the parochial house. His mind went to the dry shoes he would get into as soon as he got there, and then again to the new car which in a matter of minutes he would be guiding along the narrow, pitted dirt lane back to the tarred road and down, out of the hills.

'I hope you're in condition for the climb,' he remarked to the doctor as they passed each other.

The doctor looked up towards the house, laughed quietly and nodded in reply.

When he had passed the bridge his mind turned back to thoughts of the new car, its comfort, the pride of ownership, getting home and into dry shoes, a warm meal. Back at the farm at the end of the road he found that the doctor had parked his car in such a way that he could not get his own out. He examined the situation for a moment, slightly taken aback once more by having, unexpectedly again, lost the use of the just purchased car.

In the house he found that Sarah had neglected the fire and the black cast-iron range was lukewarm. Its tepidity made the kitchen feel even colder. The creel beside the range was empty and as he saw no other fuel anywhere in the kitchen there was no prospect of warming himself or drying his shoes. He thought of the hot tea Sarah had said she would make and which he had not wanted. There was nothing to do but wait for the doctor to get back and move his car.

His eye fell on a wrinkled copy of the *Donegal Democrat* that had been thrown hastily on a chair, pages open. He hadn't seen that week's *Democrat* yet and he picked it up gladly as a welcome way to pass the time and forget his discomfort and impatience. He drew a wicker chair to the window, the only place in the dim interior, made dimmer still by the approach of the early mid-winter evening, where there was light enough to read. Sitting down, he saw that the paper was open to the classified ads. Smoothing the pages and neatening them, he turned back to the front page, refolded the paper and started to read, scanning the page for the main items of interest.

It was last week's paper. He had read it before. In spite of that he looked at the dateline for confirmation, in disappointment. He looked around the kitchen for other reading material, but there was nothing. He tried the out of date copy of the provincial newspaper once more, but its staleness only made him the more aware of the dampness of his shoes, and he put it aside.

He looked at a calendar on the wall. It was the standard one he saw in every farm house he entered, distributed by the local sheep and cattle mart, with a colour picture of fat cows grazing green pastures in bright sun before distant blue hills. With a sense of surprise he saw that he had somehow lost a day. How could that be? He looked at the date on his watch, then back at the calendar. Examining it more carefully, he realized that it was last year's. Then he saw that Sarah had torn away the pages for the first two months, leaving the old calendar at March. In his mind he saw her sitting in the kitchen, patient through the long, dim cold winter measuring the passage of time by the calendar, until in early spring she had gone out in the finer weather to help the men with turf and crop and finally hay, forgetting the calendar and its printed days, guiding herself instead by the passing seasons themselves.

Hearing a sound from the upper room, he realized that someone was there. Going to the door of the room, he found Sarah's elderly husband convalescing in bed from a bout of flu. He greeted him and they spoke briefly. From the husband he learned that Sarah's brother, confined to the house with arthritis, was resting in the lower room. Going back through the kitchen to the door of the lower room, he conversed briefly with the brother. Since neither man seemed inclined to long conversation he went back to the wicker chair and sat down again. He thought of the new car outside, as useless as if it had broken down, and then of his walk to the house on the facing hill. He wondered how this odd piece of Donegal had remained as it had been for so long – was it, possibly, centuries? – hardly touched by modern times.

Then he thought about himself, sitting in the chilly kitchen midway between the two old men. Their oldness was like the oldness of the hills themselves, like the oldness of this place, this remaining, fading enclave of an older Ireland, of the past wedged into the present world. He glanced out the door and across the valley but saw no sign of the doctor returning. His eye went again to the newspaper and then to the out of date calendar. He resigned himself to the wait and settled back on the chair, losing himself in his thoughts. The hills, he saw, had their own time. Nothing could hurry them, certainly not the damp discomfort and impatience of a parish priest.

A KEEN OBSERVER
OF FOOTWEAR

After I sold the yellow dog I had only the black bitch with the white and tan markings. She was what they call a tricolour, mostly black, with white at the paws and on the chest, a small white diamond behind her head at the shoulder, and two tan spots over the eyes, one over each eye. The tan spots – what they call yellow in the hills – had the effect, from a little distance, of staring, intent eyes, something the sheep would see at once and which would have its effect on them, and they were the strong point of the markings in the estimation of the local farmers. The white diamond was the weak one, for the diamond should have been a full white collar generously encircling neck and throat, the mark of a good working sheep dog. But the yellow spots made up for that.

'I very seldom seen a dog with them yellow spots over the eyes,' old Nealy told me, 'but what he was a good worker.'

There were other signs too that Petey had used in picking her out to save from the rest of the litter, destined for drowning. He had looked inside the pup's mouth at the palate to see if it was black, he had inspected ears and tail and paws, and somehow read in what he saw there that this was the right pup to save. I myself came in the course of time and long days of work together to associate the yellow spots with the bitch's keen intelligence, the white diamond – or rather, lack of white collar – with what seemed to me her sometimes erratic behaviour when rounding up sheep, her wildness. Whether it really was erratic or not, as wild as I thought it was, is something I think I will never surely know, because I was almost as new to the business as she was – far newer, in fact, if you consider that she had it in the blood and I did not – and I was liable to misjudgements about all sorts of things. Training her would be, as I recognized only later, a form of training myself as well. That was the hardest thing to learn.

Looking back on it, I wonder what kind of idea I had of a dog's mind, a dog's way of seeing, and I can understand now how closed in I was by my own narrow human way of seeing, of thinking. I suppose, following the book I had on the breeding and training of sheep dogs, I saw the training of a dog as mainly a matter of discipline, mine as well as the dog's, the discipline to stick to it every day, to work at it, to develop habits, to practise, to form a routine, the training of a dog, that is, conceived in terms of training a human, training an athlete, say, or a musician. Or perhaps I, and the book with me, was too influenced by the training of circus dogs, the training in doing tricks. There is a difference between the training of a dog to do tricks and the natural working of a sheep dog. The tricks are not an inborn part of the dog's nature, are external to it, thought up by the trainer, are in every respect something invented by the master and inculcated into the dog by a system of rewards and punishments; but the working of the sheep dog is part of the dog, part of the dog's being, the dog's nature. If it was learned (and, thinking about it now, I suppose it was, once, a long time ago), it was learned many centuries ago, thousands of years before men and dogs had anything much to do with one another, learned in the wild, and learned by the dogs themselves, without instructors. We can only speculate about this, of course, but if there ever was an outside instructor who taught dogs to round up and herd animals it must have been a god who did it, or what we would call a god. Otherwise we can only talk vaguely about *nature,* about *instinct,* or accept the fact that animals, just like men, have the ability to teach themselves, to learn from experience. That at any rate seems to be the origin of the sheep dog's innate skills, skills that I mistakenly thought I had to teach my dogs, not yet understanding that I only had to give them the chance to come out and develop.

When Stub first came to the farm – for that was her name, the name I gave her, because at six weeks she was so short and stout she reminded me of a huge cigarette stub – I knew at once she would be a big dog, you could tell just looking at her. Charley, Petey's young son, who had brought her up the hill to me from his own place six miles down into the valley towards Donegal Town and the sea, only fifteen years old himself but already full of knowledge of the nature and the ways of animals, confirmed my own surmise.

'Aye, he'll make a big dog!' he said, calling the bitch 'he' because in the Donegal hills all dogs, whether dog or bitch, are 'he' or 'him', as sheep are too, both ram and ewe, and just as, conversely, all cats are 'she' or 'her'. To Charley the bigness would be a good quality, long legs and a powerful body to leap from knoll to knoll upwards on the rough slopes, speed to run out beyond fleeing sheep, head them off and bring them together into a flock, stamina of a big body to keep working on the hard up and down of the hill.

'Aye, a big dog all right,' he said. and smiled broadly, his voice warm with the same enthusiasm it had had when he said, the first time he sold me ewes, 'Them sheep's *wild*.' To me, inexperienced, or almost so, the bigness, like the wildness, seemed no advantage. Just as I had chosen 'a handy wee cow', a nicely moderate-size black cow that produced plenty of milk for her calf and us, but was not too productive, and hence not too hard to feed, not too demanding on the poor and slow-growing fodder of our high, exposed farm, so I was also looking for a handy wee dog, one that would fit into a neat, small corner of the kitchen of our small mountain house.

But when she first went out with us, with me and the yellow dog, Stub, only six weeks old, or perhaps seven, was still stout, stubby, short legged. Except for chaining or locking her up there was no way to keep her from following along with us. It was the urge to work coming out in her from the beginning, the instinctive drive to get into the action, to be useful. The rough ground I strided over in my high rubber boots and which the yellow dog took in easy leaps was more of an impediment to Stub, and there were moments when I thought I was going to have to rescue her from the worst places. I never gave in to the impulse to do so, but just looked on as she plopped unawares into some sumpy, sticky bit of wet bog, an old drain perhaps that had gone uncleared for a generation and had filled up with a mixture of gluey particles of fine bog and tough, clinging roots of coarse grass. The yellow dog and I had learned to avoid such places, he with his easy long leap, me with a more deliberate effort and planting of my feet before the jump, but Stub's attempted leaps, the first time, fell short. Her forepaws reached the more solid turf on the far side, but not the rest of her. I remember the first time I saw her immersed up to her throat in clinging mud, wondered if I should go to her aid, then decided to wait at least until I heard her anguished yelps. They never came. Instead Stub dug her claws into the solid ground her front legs had reached and tugged desperately at it, slowly pulling the rest of her thick body up and out of the mud. The yellow dog hardly looked back, eager to be on to the sheep and his work, but I stayed for a minute and watched the pup's, to me, incredible efforts, successful ones. I stayed the first few times it happened, then when I knew she would always be able to rescue herself I just left her and followed on after the yellow dog hurrying ahead of me.

It wasn't long before Stub made real my pessimistic and Charley's optimistic forecast. Her body and legs lengthened out, and within a few months I had a dog as long and lean as she had at first been short and stubby. Her name became a puzzle, since she no longer looked it, and especially to my neighbours, who were used to calling dogs by names like Rex and Rover, Daisy, Brandy, Fly, Toby, names that were 'easy got', as one of them put it – easy to remember. 'Stub' was a puzzle to them, and often became 'Spot'. Stub herself was fortunate in her exemption from any speculation about the oddity of her name. I often wondered whether she thought of it as *her* name, something she possessed, or simply as a sound, a sign that she was wanted for work or food or praise, that attention was being demanded of her, just another of the many signs and sounds I was so intent on inculcating into her consciousness.

The name was only one of the many lessons I was so systematically giving her, much as if I were determined to drive out all the by-ways of natural intelligence, replacing them with a kind of machine obedience, myself carefully obeying my own master, the book, written by some distant breeder of sheep dogs in Australia. Where he went astray I did too. In time I would lose faith in the book, all books, see them as an impediment to the unclouded mind, would lose faith as well in sheep dog trials and artificial tests of skill. In time I would hear my neighbour young John O'Neill point out that conditions on the rough heather hill were altogether different from those on a level expanse of grassland, with four or five mild-natured hornless lowland sheep, already half intimidated by having been gathered and penned and transported and further kept waiting until their moment to be the guinea pigs set aside for the attention of some expert master-dog team, expert, that is to say, in dealing with just that small number of quiet sheep on an easy terrrain. On the hill, John pointed out, the land was rougher and our breed of horned sheep was wilder, and it was not easy to put every last one of some sixty or seventy of those mountain sheep together into a flock, and then to hold them there and drive them home, in off 'the wild hills' where they had perhaps been grazing unmolested for half the summer – 'away on the wild hills entirely'. A little wildness was wanted in the dog to match the wildness of the sheep and of the hill, John said. The rules of the sheep dog trials would be out of place there.

John's comment set me thinking again, and tempered my faith in the book. Still, without experience, or with very little of it, I was largely dependent on what I could find in the book. So the daily systematic ten-minute training sessions went on morning and afternoon, with lessons in coming to foot, and sitting down, and going out left or right, and in waiting. Stub patiently put up with all that teaching, quickly learning and assimilating whatever I wanted her to, there in front of the house, that is, but on the hill with the sheep her own methods always reasserted themselves.

I saw later that had I followed the counsel of some of my oldest neighbours, who told me simply: 'Let the dog work the sheep . . . Let the dog work the sheep', and controlled my impulse to well-meant but ill-advised interference, she would have taught herself as she went. She would have learned, as I see now, from her own instinct, from that long store of ancestral experience she carried with her in her blood. For it is that that makes a sheepdog, not the master's clever training but the generations and generations, many centuries or millennia back, of running in packs, of working together to scent out and track down and find flocks and herds of prey, and then working in unison, leader and pack, to round up and hold and finally to kill. All that self-training that made survival in the wild possible had developed the qualities in Stub's blood that I wanted to put to work for myself, that I would then take credit for and be so proud of when it did work for me. I would ignore the fact that I was a latecomer taking advantage of something that had developed, evolved, precisely because I was not there to interfere with it, stop it.

On the hill Stub was wild – or so it seemed to me, because she wasn't following the book rules as closely as I wanted her to. In the house she was quiet and obedient. The house involved a significant but less formal part of her training. Actually, there was a thatched craw just beyond the house, near the byre and sheds, and Stub spent her nights there, out where she could sleep in the open air. But there is nothing, it seems, which is not part of the training of a dog. Everything has its influence. Following the book, I made a point of chaining Stub up just to get her used to the chain, 'used to restraint', as the author put it. I remember her horror when, about eight weeks old, she suddenly discovered this limitation on her freedom of movement, that she could no longer come and go about the farm street as she liked, frightening hens when the mood took her, boldly facing up to the rooster when he came to the defence of the hens, or testing one of the cats for playfulness, and generally running about on little journeys of discovery. What made her first experience of the chain so grim for Stub, apart from the fact that it was the first and totally unprepared for by any instruction or limitation beforehand, was that she had no idea what it was that was holding her. The chain that she had so quietly submitted to did not yet have any concrete meaning for her, and even after it had caught her up she would run to its limit with all her normal energy and speed, much as if it were not there, or as if another try might make it not there (so little could she accept this new fact), as if it were some invisible accident that would be overcome by a simple energetic repetition of the – until then – normal kind of activity. Watching her hurl herself to the full length of the chain, to be caught up short by it and flop tail first in the direction of the thrust, then run back to the craw and out again to the length of the chain, I was at first alarmed, distressed, then less so when I saw she was not going to hurt herself. It was part of her sturdiness.

In a short while Stub had accepted the inevitable, her master's superior dark cunning. In the long run, later on when she was full grown, she would one day demonstrate that she continued to accept the chain only out of docility, and could slip it, or even break it, when she felt strongly enough about the matter. But that belongs to another part of the story.

To get Stub used to restraint I took to keeping her chained

up to her craw most of the time, at first, and I would have kept that up had not Peadar Nohar More stopped by one evening and questioned my procedure.

'You keep the dog in the craw always?' he asked. It was a question, but a comment too. I knew Peadar well enough to know that it was the prelude to some piece of instruction, and I knew myself just well enough to know that I would resist Peadar's instruction for a while (citing the book, perhaps, silently, to myself) and then yield, follow his advice.

I nodded.

'Better for you to keep him in here, with you,' Peadar instructed.

Pointless discussing with Peadar my book-acquired theories about training the dog to the chain. Pointless also going into my lingering sense that the proper place for farm dogs is in the yard, not the kitchen. The kitchen, the most important room in the house, was in my eyes meant for people, not animals. A theory not accepted in the thatched houses of the Blue Stacks, where there was often a dog for every man, and several men to every house, and dogs and men together, in from the hill perhaps and several hours of mist or rain, all in the kitchen, steaming by the fire, the men their clothes, the dogs their fur. In the small-farm, largely moneyless economy of the hills the unspoken but pervasive atmosphere of democracy that extended from farmer to farmer was reflected in the way a man felt about and treated his dog as well. 'Democracy' is a poor word for it. It is something more profound, an awareness that an animal has sense, reason not unlike human powers of reasoning, and feelings not unlike human feelings: pride, vanity. It is a sense that human and animal life are part of a continuum, that we are basically all one. It was a sense of things I still lacked.

I would have quietly resisted Peadar's urging to bring Stub into the house and install her on a sack in the kitchen had it not been for one remark he made which had a telling, decisive effect on me.

'If you keep the dog outside, how is he going to learn?' he asked, then quickly reiterated his point: 'If you keep him outside, I'm saying, how is he going to learn what you're saying to him?'

'Learn?' I echoed. 'She gets training every day.'

'Aye, and you're right too, to take him out among the sheep

every day and walk through them with him at your heel, coaxing him and talking to him until he gets used with them, gently. You're right to do that,' Peadar repeated, in preparation, I knew, for further remarks. I knew too that we were getting further and further apart in our intent, for my sessions of training Stub were not walks through the flock, but were more classroom style on the unpaved street in front of the house, with repetitions of commands to sit down or lie down, or to come to foot. They were more a matter of teacher and pupil, or master and servant, than the free partnership of man and dog that Peadar had in mind.

Peadar paused, then resumed. 'I'm saying, when the dog be lying there in the corner on the sack, he'll be listening to every word you're saying. That's the way he learns, you see.'

Peadar's remark was a hint of another kind of training, a more important kind.

So Stub moved into the house, for a good part of the time anyway. Nights were still spent in the craw. It quickly became clear that she liked to be out there at night, for she was restless when we kept her inside, and in the small hours of the morning would wake and shift about and paw her sack, uneasy. When I started chaining her out again at night she showed her preference for the open air as a place to sleep by jumping up when she saw me get up from my chair and running eagerly ahead of me in the darkness and on up to the craw, where she stood patiently while I put the collar around her neck and then clipped the long chain to that. So accustomed did she become to sleeping out in the open that she went right through the snowy nights of winter there. In the house, too, her corner of the kitchen was the furthest from the fire I could make it. It was not harshness on my part. Local lore had it that a dog that lay near the fire would stiffen up – 'take the pains'. Stub stayed away from artificial heat, her body made its own heat, and she grew hardy and resistant to wet and cold.

The unconscious training that took place in the house was something else. It was training that was going on without my thinking about it. Little instructions to the dog, like calling her to come inside, into the house, while I stood by the open kitchen door waiting to close it after her – 'Come in, come in!' – which later would be repeated without thought on the hill working the sheep, only there it would have a different meaning: *Come in to me, to my foot!* Learned at the house, it was followed on the hill. 'Come in, come in!' I would call, and Stub would come around the flock towards me, so that they would move on ahead, away from both of us. It was a manoeuvre of driving sheep instead of gathering them. There were other moments when I told her to go out of the house, and the command 'Go on out!' became on the hill the signal to run out around a group of sheep and bring them together. My two most important commands to Stub thus developed unconsciously, between ourselves, arising out of our natural habits, our talking together, as it were. Unconsciously, automatically I gestured when I called to her, waving one arm or the other in the direction I had in mind for her to go, or perhaps snapping my fingers, left hand or right one, as I had seen my neighbours do when they wanted their dogs to run out and cap some sheep.

A whistle was added to the vocabulary. At first I suppose it was an automatic way of calling the dog. Later it evolved into a sign to her to change direction. I don't know how that came about. Perhaps it was because coming in to your master's whistle implies changing direction, coming to him instead of going away, and as Stub by instinct moved around the flock in a gathering motion, and avoided running into and through them, the whistle simply made her change the direction of her long running arc on the other side of the flock from me. When I wanted her to stay moving back and forth that way on the other side of the flock and bring them towards me I found myself using a series of short soft whistles. At each sound from me Stub turned sharply and ran back the other way, until the pattern was established, and I called out some conventional word or phrase of encouragement and approval, 'Good dog!' perhaps, 'Good dog!'

But Stub learned by her very nature. The ability to learn, to deduce, basic to survival in the wild, carried over in her blood into the tame conditions of domesticity. She learned all sorts of things about me I would never have thought to teach her, because I did not know them about myself. Her early hard experience trying to keep up with the yellow dog and me when she was a pup had developed powerful muscles in her legs which served her well later on. When running out after sheep she could leap long distances from knoll to knoll, barely pausing on the far side to get her footing before resuming her rapid running gait. When she was on some particularly rough ground where the heather was deep or where high rushes hid our view of each other, Stub used her powerful hind legs to jump high into the air, and I would see her appear vertically, her body straight up and down, her head and neck stretched to their full extent upward, her front paws folded and hanging limp before her chest, her entire body appearing above dense clumps of rushes that were three or four feet high, seeming to be suspended there at the height of her jump, her eyes intent in my direction, looking for some visual signal from me.

I carried a long hazel walking stick when we were out on the hill together, and that became my signalling device as I held it out in one direction or another to indicate to Stub which way I wanted her to go. For at such times, with her view obstructed by the vegetation, it was often easier for me to see the sheep at a distance than for her to find them from close up. Then my signals guided her to them. Of course, the reverse often happened too, when I lost track of the sheep, or was not even aware that they were there in the first place, stray sheep sheltering behind some overhanging bank of turf perhaps and thus hidden from sight, and Stub would find them by herself and bring them into view.

The remarkable thing about our system of hazel stick signals was that it worked not only for signalling right and left (and yet I often marvelled at the dog's ability to interpret the slant of the stick and translate it into a direction, even at distances of a hundred or a hundred and fifty yards) but also when I wanted Stub to move back and away from me. Then I held the stick neither to right nor left but either directly in front of me and straight up into the air, or else in the direction of some specific sheep, one that we had missed, and that was out beyond the rest of the flock. It was something I did without thought, in the heat of the moment, but she understood the gesture from the start, and would turn and race away from me with a wonderfully precise interpretation of the direction I wanted her to go. I always felt a kind of renewed surprise when I saw her do that, and pleasure.

It took me a long time – in retrospect I see how slow I was – to realize that Stub had caught on to the system of semi-rotational grazing we were gradually introducing as we progressively fenced our land. I say 'system' but in fact for a long time we were only feeling our way into a system, as the new fences slowly stretched out along the hill and closed in sections of the farm. The first area fenced was six acres, but that was for the sake of hay, a meadow, not primarily for pasture. That was the 'park'. The second was twelve acres, and included a stretch of rough heather hill. We called it the 'hill paddock', but that was not mainly intended for grazing either, but as a place to gather and hold the sheep when we wanted them together, when we were getting ready to dose or dip them and were waiting for a day, rare in winter, that was both dry and free from frost, or in November when we were putting the ram out to the ewes and wanted them in a small area to save him from having to wander long distances over the hills looking for the ones that were in heat on any given day of the seventeen-day cycle.

The fence that held the ewes together for the ram also kept the ram in on his own territory and away from encounter with other rams, encounter that in the mating season could become a confrontation fatal to one or the other, and at the least damaging to both. Five months later, in April, when the heavy ewes were near their time to lamb, the ten acre paddock served our purpose by keeping them in a small area, away from the open hill, so that we could go through them once or twice a day, find the ones that had lambed and then patiently coax the ewe – it was ever so slow a process – to lead her newborn lamb down on to the soft green meadow-grass nearer in to the house.

Having sheep grazing those fenced-in areas for only part of the time and off them for longer periods, we noticed after a while how the grass or heather on that ground recovered quicker and became denser, seeming to have profited from the alternating periods of heavy grazing, and hence good manuring, and then being saved. It was, perhaps, a concrete lesson in the ancient idea of the sabbath, the cyclical recurring period of total idleness, of rest and vacancy, recovery. That spurred us on to fence the hill itself, a long project that took years, and gave us two more large areas for grazing, the smaller part of it all that area of the farm that was below the road, down to the curragh and lake, half overgrown with thick reeds, that bounded the lower part of our land; the larger part the long open expanse above the road running up and over the crest of the hill, the long ridge of the lower Blue Stacks, and down again to the swift small stream at the back pouring rapidly and noisily out of the higher hills.

It was all going on while Stub was getting used to working sheep. As we fenced, our system of grazing evolved slowly. We were always in the process of slow experimentation, changing to meet the varying condition of the land, or to try new ideas, and so I was not aware of anything like a system developing. Stub was. Her work would have been easier for her had I been as alert in that respect as she was. With my usual underestimation of Stub's intelligence, the fixed prejudice of my own mind that I had been brought up with and that told me that the minds of animals functioned on instinct, not reasoning, I did not think to look for any signs of Stub's perceiving the system of grazing that was evolving for our newly fenced areas. I was just casual and haphazard enough to be unaware of any system myself. Decisions were made according to the occasion. The routine changed monthly, sometimes weekly. There was an air of improvisation about it, while we were gaining experience.

How then did I realize, finally, that Stub herself was aware of a system, or at least was looking for one? Lacking words, her major means of communication was a silent one: looking. Looking, and endless patience. When Stub wanted to communicate something, to tell me something, she would sit looking patiently at me until I finally saw that she had something on her mind. Then it was up to me to deduce what it was she wanted. Sometimes she could express that with a kind of sign language, like running over to the kitchen door two or three times and putting her nose to the crack. Other times she simply sat and stared at the door itself until it was opened. The most difficult communications were when what she had to tell me was too abstract for body signals.

It was when we were shifting sheep from one fenced section to another (in the fall of the year we often used a system of putting them down on the clean meadow aftergrass in the morning then back on to the heather in the evening), or driving newly purchased sheep to the farm, or bringing back strays. I have no idea how long, how many times, Stub looked at me for the signal, the command I never gave her, or why it was that one day I took her patient questioning look more seriously. Perhaps it was something in the restless course of her running out and returning again, or the precise moments in that curving course when she would leap straight into the air and, hanging there for that instant of vertical immobility, look at me for a sign. When I understood, it was obvious.

Having fenced the land into closed areas, we had in the process introduced a system of gates. There were four gates, two above the road and two below it, two near the house and two further away. It never occurred to me to name the gates and get the dog used to the names. Instead of one simple command I complicated our work by reducing everything to a series of small instructions. (Perhaps I could blame the book for this lack of insight on my part, its failure to let me know that the dog would do what was required if she only knew my intention. I think I had better blame myself.)

One day, when my mind was ready for the insight, I saw that Stub had the gates in mind when she gave me those questioning looks. She had deduced, from her experience of the way we worked the sheep, that they were meant for one or another of the gates. As soon as she knew which section of hill the sheep were destined for she took over and did the rest without commands from me. When she had gathered them to the gate I only had to go up ahead and open it. She drove them through, turning back when the last one was in, her jaws open, her tongue out, to give me a look of satisfaction.

That must have been the beginning of my respect – genuine respect – for Stub, but in spite of my occasional flashes of insight my mind remained closed to a real understanding of the dog. I think I simply did not want to see, did not want to be shaken loose in the precarious structure of my way of seeing her and myself, and the nature of our co-operation. If Stub could think things out as well as or better than I could, then who was the master, the boss, the leader of the operation, of the pack? It was probably that fear that kept me from opening my mind to discovery.

My experience of driving sheep to the mart should have changed that. I think it did to some extent. The marts did not begin until September, then they went on at regular weekly intervals until the end of October, two months out of the twelve when you had your only chance to sell your sheep. Other months there was no demand or trade. That particular year the first mart came in late August, then there was an interval of two weeks until the twelfth of September. Since prices were good at the first mart, the late August one, a lot of farmers had sheep ready to sell at the second mart, which they expected to be in a week's time, and there was a certain amount of puzzlement and impatience when it was announced for two weeks later instead of one. I was one of the impatient ones.

In summer the days are so long that the last light of one merges into the first light of the next as the sun slides slowly down behind the hills to the north, its last rays shining on the back of the house and into the kitchen through the north-facing window, but by September they are getting short: mornings are getting late and evenings approach early. Lulled by the ease of the long summer days, the early light and the late evenings, this sudden shortening of the days always took me by surprise in my first years in the hills. I was never quite prepared for it, never readjusted quickly enough beforehand.

We were nine miles from the mart, our road unpaved, difficult to get over even with a tractor. I had too many sheep for a tractor-load anyway. I decided to drive the sheep to the mart on foot, with Stub. Some of my neighbours were still doing that. We were so far from town that the only way was to start out the day before and rest overnight half way, finishing the trip in the early morning of the day of the mart itself. For me that meant driving the sheep down to Petey's at a leisurely pace, not pushing them too hard, leaving them there in a shed and going home as it was getting dark, then up before dawn and back to Petey's again in the dark, waking Charley, getting the sheep on the road by first light and along the remaining five miles to Donegal. Charley went ahead of the flock and I went behind to wave or signal warnings to traffic that there were sheep just ahead of them over the next crest or around the next sharp bend of the winding hill road. Stub seemed to understand the whole business at once, and moved busily back and forth behind the flock, keeping them on the road.

The sheep grazed the long grass along the side of the road as they went. I remember coming over the crest of a hill and seeing Donegal Town just ahead of us, two miles further down in the valley to the south, in the early light, beyond it the sky, the fields, and the distant mountains, one of them flat like a table, another, nearer the sea, scooped out like a bowl at its western end, but all of them, beyond the green and yellow and dull red-brown of the fields, the same uniform blue-grey, the cool colour of the tranquil hills, untroubled, unchanging. A slight mist hung over the low roofs of the town, held stiller by the haze of turf smoke from the early fires. We descended the last stretch of hill. The mart was on our side of the town, and so we turned off the main road just where we encountered the first dwellings and drove the sheep through a kind of residential suburb of small two-storey houses. It was an odd sensation shepherding a flock along regular town roads and streets instead of out on the open hill, a sensation of being out of place. One or two early householders opened their front doors and stood watching us pass.

In spite of our earliness the mart was already crowded with sheep when we arrived. I learned later that the aluminum-tubing pens had been more than half full of them the night before. Others had been arriving since first light. Mine were some of the last to get in, crowded into one of the last available pens with two or three other lots. As we finished driving them in I was given a numbered ticket indicating my place in the sequence of sales. Then I noticed trucks and tractors with trailers waiting outside the mart gates, their lines beginning to fill the large unpaved gravel parking lot. Men who had already left their sheep in the mart, and were standing outside watching others arrive, commented on the large numbers there were for such an early hour. Some thought it was going to be a record mart for numbers of sheep sold.

It was about seven-thirty, and there was nothing to do until the mart began at twelve. Four and a half hours. But that was only to be the beginning of my wait that day, for my sheep were far back in line. It meant, as nearly as I could find out from asking some of the men standing about, a wait of ten or twelve hours.

'If you're lucky,' one of them added.

'Oh aye,' another commented, seeing my surprise, 'the mart could go on to midnight.'

I wondered how I was going to spend that time. My heavy boots and old farm clothes would not be entirely out of place in one of the hotel lounges, they were used enough to farmers on mart days, but I wondered about Stub. There was also a sense of uncertainty in my mind about leaving the sheep. Were they safe? I wondered. Although the available space within the mart had been filled, there was still a restless activity inside. Men were coming and going along the aisles between the rows of pens and rearranging groups of sheep, snagging them one by one out of the pen they were in and moving them to another pen closer to the auction ring. I noticed someone going through the sheep in the pen where mine were. He picked out a ewe and dragged her by the horn out of the pen. Looking at the sheep, I saw that they had already become mixed up so that mine were dispersed among those of other farmers, and I found it impossible to count them. I decided I had better stay with them, for the time being at least, until the activity quieted down. In that expectation I was deceived, the activity growing instead of subsiding as the morning grew brighter.

Although overcast the day was dry, but I soon felt my feet growing uncomfortably cold. Looking down at my leather boots, I realized that in spite of the dryness of the weather I was standing in a pool of wetness and muck. It was my first indication of the fact that the mart sewage system, overtaxed by the unexpected number of animals, was not equal to the load, so that the concrete floors of the pens were gradually filling up with a brown liquid mixture of urine and droppings. In my concern about the sheep I had not noticed it before, but now I saw that it was already up above the top of the thick soles and heels of my boots. It had been accumulating during the night, and I realized uneasily that the sheep too were standing in it, motionless, too crowded together to move about, without fodder – in short, without any means of keeping warm. Throughout the morning and the long afternoon, I would notice that the thickening muck gradually splashed on to everything around, on to my clothes, my hands, the aluminum tubes of the pens, and on to the sheep as well, so that their fleeces, so clean on the hill with its fresh rainfalls and open winds, became a kind of splotched, dirty colour, and though the day was dry they themselves looked wetter and wetter, and poorer and poorer as sheep, as their fast took effect and their sides, usually swelling out gracefully at that time of the year with the still abundant grass, got flatter and duller with hunger and damp. The sheep that had looked so good on the hill looked so poor then, crowded there in the mart pens, reduced from living things to merchandise, the fringes of their wool a wet brown of dung and piss.

By the middle of the morning I wanted to get away from it all for a short break, a cup of tea and an egg, or some toast. I suddenly remembered that in my haste to get the sheep on the road as early as possible I had simply skipped breakfast. I looked around for a face that I recognized, someone who might have his own sheep in a pen near mine and whom I could ask to keep an eye on mine while Charley and I went to a cafe for something to eat, but saw no one I knew. I suggested to Charley that he should go home and get some more sleep, but with a kind of loyalty he decided against it.

'I'm all right,' he said.

There was nothing to do but stand about and wait, with Stub always at my feet. We took turns going for tea, and I sent Charley first. Waiting for my turn, my own impatience became more burdensome as I noticed other men standing near me quietly observing the immobile sheep packed nose to tail in the pens: when they lifted their eyes from the sheep and looked about there was nothing restless in the look, none of the futile impatience I felt; nor was there even a look of patience. The expression on their faces was simply a neutral one. I did not realize at the time that this mart that was so unappealing to me was a kind of day out for them, a day away from the farm, not unlike the fair-days they had been used to before the mart was founded.

The mart itself, I saw, even took on some of the characteristics of the old fairs it had replaced. Long before the sales in the auction ring were due to start a steady bargaining and trading, buying and selling was going on along the aluminum rails, and as the bargaining went on in the style of the fair sheep were continually being taken out of the pens they were in and put in elsewhere. Out in the gravel parking lot the same thing had started among the trucks and trailers full of sheep.

The incessant activity before the actual opening of the mart puzzled me, the more so as not all the sheep being moved were ones there had been any dealings over. After the auctions started whole flocks were moved up from where they had been put when they arrived to pens closer in to the ring that were becoming vacant, so that some men, those who could manage it, came late but got their sheep in early. The continual moving about of sheep caused a confusion about the pens and in the aisles that became worse when the sales themselves began. The spaces that served as aisles led to the ring on one side and away from it on the other. A series of gates closed them off into sections, so that sheep could be brought up in groups, one group at a time, and fed into the ring that way. An orderly system. Thus once a man had his sheep all together and out of the pen into the aisle he would have nothing more to do but herd them along gate by gate and section by section until they were on the weigh-bridge that came immediately before the auction ring. That was what I thought, standing there impatiently that morning waiting for sales to begin.

The actuality was something else. The system, so well designed for an orderly handling of animals, was not a match for the casual ways men develop on remote and sparsely settled hills. When the sales were on and the sheep were being moved up there seemed to be continual counter-movements or cross-currents of other sheep, and gates that should have been closed turned out to be open, or the other way around, so that there were shouts of 'Close that gate!' or 'Cap that yoe ahead – bring her back!' and a good deal of waving of arms as men ran out to bring back the escaped sheep. In the end it seemed four processes were going on at once, all in the same space. While some men were moving sheep up towards the ring to put them in for sale, others were bringing sheep they had just bought away from the ring and towards the mart gates to take them out, or heading them for vacant pens where they would be kept until their owner had arranged transportation for them, while others still were busy shifting their sheep from one pen to another, and a fourth category were those who were bargaining and buying and selling right at the pens, in the fashion of the fair. Those bartered sheep were then shifted as well.

I contemplated inwardly the trouble this lack of system would mean for me when I came to bring my own sheep up to the ring, and I looked for signs that things might settle down into a pattern, an orderly routine as the day progressed. In that too I was disappointed, for the activity only seemed to grow. Troublesome as all this was for the farmers involved, I gradually saw how hard it was on the sheep themselves, the abuse they suffered from the combined crowding, moving about and confusion. The spectacle of their dung- and piss-flecked fleeces as they left the pens was depressing; more so was the sight of sheep that had been injured in the crush. Some had broken legs, and were thus suddenly greatly reduced in value and saleability. Those sheep were separated from the rest of their lot, in order to avoid bringing down the price of the others, and sold on their own, hobbling around the ring on three legs and attracting a few shillings, graphic examples of the hazards of the mart for the animals themselves. The most depressing thing I saw in the mart, though, was a dead ewe lamb, left behind in one of the pens, crushed to death and trampled down by the larger sheep too densely crowded in around it, the flat body half indistinguishable in the brown muck it was lying in.

As often happens, one confusion sometimes attracts another. Stepping outside the mart about noon, just when sales were due to begin but in fact showed no signs of doing so, I found a loose crowd of men and boys standing around a small van near the entrance to the parking lot. A farmer from somewhere on one of the remote and sparsely populated hill roads to the south of Donegal Town had brought in large mature ewes, overcrowded, evidently, in the limited space of his small van and without enough air for the time they were kept in it. He had planned to unload them immediately upon arrival, then had been stopped at the gates of the already full mart, and had lost time looking for some way to let them out and yet keep them together, not having foreseen the necessity of bringing along tying-rope or, having found that, perplexed by the problem of where to tie them, what to tie them to. When at last he opened the van doors to let the sheep out he found them asphyxiated, or semi-asphyxiated and in a dying condition. Perhaps some of them were already dead then, I could not tell.

When I came upon them the first thing I saw was the van with two or three dead or dying ewes (they were a good breed of large four-year-olds and would have brought a good price) hanging down the sides of the van by their hind legs, their throats cut as if they had been slaughtered, the red blood draining through the gashes. The farmer, seeing them dead or almost so, had made a quick decision to 'slaughter' them, then to sell them as carcasses, as mutton, to one of the local butchers, rather than merely let them die, in which case they would be carrion and the meat not fit for use. More of his sheep were hanging from the chain-wire fence that marked the limits of the mart grounds. The intention was to drain the foul blood from their bodies while there was still some remnant of circulation left in their systems. It was a gruesome sight, the living red blood flowing down from the opened throats over the black and white heads and dripping thickly, semi-clotted in heavy pools in the yellow gravel below. Men and boys stood around silently, occasionally exchanging some hardly voiced comment. Other sheep from the same van were lying on the ground gasping convulsively for breath, irregularly, with long intervals between each gasp, raising their heads blindly from time to time in a kind of flailing motion.

It was all the other side, the shadow side, of sheep farming. The sheep that looked so well on the green slopes of the high farms, grazing peacefully before the calm, unmoving backdrop of the blue hills, had here become elements of trade, pieces of merchandise without other value than their market price. I remember my feelings of regret, and puzzlement too, at having treated my sheep so well throughout the entire year, in some cases several years, to expose them to this indignity on the final day of my ownership. It seemed to me a kind of treason, an admission that all the peaceful grazing and good care was for the worst of motives.

Stub, who had never been to a fair or a mart before, had never in fact been further from the farm than the post office-general store in Letterbarrow a few miles south of us, seemed to understand the whole matter better than I did, responded more professionally by taking everything in her stride. From the time we got near the mart grounds and began meeting other flocks being brought in, she saw at once the necessity of keeping our sheep separate from the others. She kept up a continuous busy movement until all our sheep were safely in. Then she was as reluctant as I was to leave them unattended, turning back whenever I left the pen, clearly torn between the desire to stay with me and the opposing one of staying with the sheep. Even when I took a break and went to a cafe for something to eat Stub showed her manners, staying at my heels until I was seated, then quietly curling up at my feet under the table, stirring only when I gave her some food from my own meal.

The auctioneer's quick soft chant of numbers started about an hour after noon, and the sales began. At first prices seemed good, and I felt a surge of optimism. Then, within the first sixty minutes, prices began to slacken. The comments of the farmers sitting on the tiered wooden benches that surrounded the auction ring were made in general terms, sounded as if they applied to the whole state of the market, but were only the way of referring to single transactions. If a lot of sheep went a particularly good price there would be a surge of chuckling and someone would say, 'Sheep prices are good the day!'; but when, shortly afterwards, another lot, not much different in quality, failed to sell, another comment was heard: 'It's a poor day for sheep' – with falling intonation, sadly. Gradually it was the second opinion that became more general and finally prevailed. The good early sales had reflected the presence of a few men eager to buy. When they – there were three or four of them at the most – had got their own supply, perhaps fifty or sixty young sheep in each case, and were no longer bidding against one another, the mart was left to a few professional merchants who were experienced enough and cautious enough to avoid pushing up the prices against themselves by too much competitive bidding.

As the day went on prices dropped steadily lower. At last they reached so low a level that men stopped selling, simply standing on the weigh-bridge listening, as though in deep thought, in meditation, to the auctioneer's chant, the final slightly drawn out number that indicated the highest bid received, and then, in the pause of silence, quietly shook their heads, ever so slightly, almost imperceptibly, to be quickly interpreted by the auctioneer's rapid, 'No sale.' That comment itself took on an increasing sound of disappointment, as more and more lots were taken back out of the ring unsold, to be returned to their farms for another fortnight, then to be brought to the mart again for another try.

The situation became preoccupying for me, for prices had dropped below the level where it would be reasonable for me to sell my animals, or so I thought. Talking to some of my neighbours, young men who themselves had brought in a large number of sheep, I heard their opinion of what had happened. There had been no mart at all for two weeks, contrary to normal expectations, and farmers who had been encouraged by the good prices marked up at the first mart of the season, the one at the end of August, had been impatient to get some of their sheep to the second mart, to take advantage of the demand. That ready supply of stock had increased when the next week's mart had been skipped, hence the extra large supply – 'twicet what you would be looking for', was the way they put it – that had gathered at this mart. Still, that did not account for the very low prices. That was another matter. It seemed that this mart coincided with the annual harvest fair over the hills in the next glen northward, at Glenties, the last of the large harvest fairs in our region. It was held regularly on the twelfth of September, and was a major social occasion too, in addition to its importance as a sheep fair. I had been there the year before, and remembered that it had attracted farmers from all parts of the county, and merchants from all the northern and western part of the country. While the farmers on our side of the hills had all brought their sheep to the Donegal mart, as they had in the past always taken them to the Donegal fair, the buyers had all gone to the bigger event in Glenties. Hence there were only two or three men buying sheep at the mart.

As the day went on I began to think about taking my sheep home again to wait for another mart, when prices might be better. As fewer and fewer sheep were actually sold I made more and more mental comparisons between sheep in the ring that had not attracted a high enough price to persuade their owner to let them go, and my own sheep, looking ever poorer, in my eyes at least, as their fleece grew dirtier and more matted and their sides seemed flatter, their bodies hungrier and more meagre. I would walk from the ring to the pen where the sheep were, inspect them yet another time, then back to the ring for another comparison. The problem was made greater by the lack of transportation. I thought of getting the sheep loaded on to a trailer and getting them that way at least as far as the end of the asphalt road, within three miles of home anyway, but when I started to ask around among the tractor men outside the mart in the parking lot I found that it was almost impossible to get a tractor that was free to do the work. The lack of sales meant that almost all the tractors that had come in the morning loaded with sheep were still loaded with them, and those few that had emptied their load were more than booked for the rest of the day and well into the night. It meant that I would have to

97

drive the sheep home as I had driven them in, or else leave them standing overnight in the wet muck of the cold pens, fasting, having fasted, by the following morning, for twenty-four hours.

It was not only concern for the sheep, but concern for what I felt was my own property that intensified my worry. I had often heard my neighbours talk about the dangers of marts for sheep and the necessity to at once dose and dip any sheep that had been there, as a precaution against inner and outer parasites, worms and fluke in the first case, ticks and lice in the second. More than one of them had told me: 'If you take sheep to the mart, don't bring them home again!' Looking at the sheep then, seeing them as I had never seen them before in all the time they grazed the hill, I thought of that advice. There was no alternative, however, and I was aware that if I waited too long in taking them out darkness would make it impossible for me to drive them home. Even dusk would involve the risk of losing at least some of them.

At about five o'clock I decided to take them out. That too was a problem, one more to be faced in this long day. First came snagging them out of the pen one by one and gathering them in the aisle, a task that would have been relatively simple if that section of the aisle could have been kept free for the ten or fifteen minutes I needed, but the confusion along the ramps meant that I was never sure whether sheep we had just pulled out were staying in the aisle or being moved on with other groups of sheep passing through. Stub did her best to help, but the confined space cramped her, frustrated her movements. In the end Charley stayed outside the pen keeping them together while I went through the sheep in the pen and pulled my own out one by one. Getting them herded along to the mart gates was slightly less difficult, with Charley ahead and me behind, the system we had used on the road coming in, but once through the gates the unexpected, but inevitable happened: the hungry sheep that went through first while I was still lagging behind at the end of the flock, and with Stub at my feet, those first sheep through bolted away for the nearest green area they could see, or perhaps smell.

Next to the parking lot on the town side of the mart was an overgrown empty lot where a good deal of rubbish and scrap metal had been dumped, with tall grass growing wild in among the refuse. It was separated from the gravel parking lot by a tall, thin scraggly hedge, and was at a lower level than it, perhaps three feet lower. When I got the final sheep through the gates and brought them together into a flock I realized that ten or twelve were missing. Neither could I see Charley. Not having noticed the old overgrown lot before I thought that some of the sheep had dashed ahead the way I myself was planning to go, along the road home, and had visions of Charley heroically trying to keep them together even without a dog. My first impulse was to follow as quickly as possible along the road to catch up with him. I stood there for a moment, uncertain. Then a man I did not recognize, but who knew me, came up to me and showed me where the sheep had gone.

With an effort Charley and Stub and I rounded up the dozen sheep that were tearing ravenously at the long wild grass of the empty lot, at the same time trying to restrain the ones that had stayed with me. It meant plenty of extra running and darting about for Stub, and made me realize that I had not stopped to ask myself how her energy would hold out over the ten uphill miles homeward. Finally, we got the flock gathered and under control and on the road, but at the first large green field we came to, still within the town limits, the sheep quickly pushed open the gate, which was not well secured, and poured rapidly in to the waiting grass. More work for Stub. It was my first realization that one of us, Charley or I, would have to try to stand at every gate and gap we passed on the way home, at least until the sheep had got something into them by grazing the grass along the sides of the road. I had not calculated on these extra delays, and I realized uneasily that at the rate we were moving it would be far after dark by the time I got the flock back to Meenaguse. There was no time to think about that, however, the main thing was to keep moving towards home.

Stub and I had already walked nine miles that day, and fifteen within the last twenty-four hours, but it was in reality more than that for her, moving back and forth as she did to keep the sheep herded together along the road, and to keep them moving. The trip home would be another nine miles for me, possibly twice that for Stub, or even three times. I had no way of knowing. Now her habit of not sparing herself when she worked, of not economizing motion and effort, would tell against her. I wondered how she would last on the return into the hills, moving steadily upwards this time, instead of descending as we had in the morning. Perhaps if I had thought all that out before leaving the mart I would have taken the chance of leaving the sheep overnight where they were, depending on their inbred hardiness to get them through. Once on the road, though, I could not again change my mind.

Slowly we ascended into the hills, the ascent itself adding to the fatigue of the day to make the trip just that much harder than the morning's descent from the hills to the town. The sheep tore hungrily at the grass and bushes of the verges or, in spite of our efforts, broke into fields through the improvised barriers of sticks and old bedsteads that took the place of gates, and had to be driven out and back with the rest of the flock again. Charley had stayed loyally with us all day, and at his turn-off (he showed no sign of taking it) I told him Stub and I would easily manage the sheep from there on. I would have welcomed his help, and his instinct for the ways of sheep, but it would have meant four more miles into the hills for him and then five miles home again. Too much, I thought.

At Ardban, another mile along, we started the real ascent into the foothills of the Blue Stacks, always marked for me by the onset of the hill breeze, the slight wind that was never absent above that point in the road, and which I had gradually learned not to regard, as I did at first, as an annoyance, but instead as a welcome return to air that was even fresher than the air only a few miles below in the valley. Now the breeze meant that we were on the last few miles back to the farm. With the coming of the breeze we also entered a stretch of rolling, reddish bogland, treeless, and even without electric wires or poles of any kind. All those were left behind, with the last trees, at the final houses along the road at Ardban. In the failing light the reddening heather was even darker. It was dusk.

My preoccupations gradually faded as dusk came on. The sheep moved slowly upward, refusing now to be kept to the road but spreading out across the bog, grazing as they went the coarse brown-red grass they were accustomed to. It seemed harder to move them on, and Stub seemed to be doing even more running backward and forward behind them, but I felt it was pointless to worry about the outcome of the day. The fading light lasted much longer than I expected it to as our eyes grew accustomed to the increasing dimness, then darkness of the evening.

About a mile beyond Ardban I realized that while I was aware of the dirt road beneath my feet and just ahead of me, I could no longer detect any of the sheep. My eyes adapted well enough to the dim light to pick up glints from the small pools of water lying in the road or sense the difference between the grass of the verge and the gravel of the road. But I had no sense of where the sheep were, could not see any of them, or Stub, could only hear an occasional movement, the sound of an animal moving through the low heather, a bleat from time to time, without knowing whether it was one of my sheep or the sheep grazing the farms we were moving through. Occasionally I heard the distinctive sound of Stub running, her paws on the gravel of the road or slapping the areas of bare, heatherless turf in the bog, or her breathing, by then laboured and heavy and audible.

At last we got to the farm, the march marked for me, as always, by the never absent round puddle of water in a low spot between the two adjacent farms, so often a cause of annoyance, now become a sign of welcome. Slowly we took the final few hundred yards of upward slope to the house and the field gate beyond. Though I could not see anything but the gravel of the road I somehow felt that the sheep were all together. I went ahead and opened the gate to the field, hoping that Stub would put them in and calling instructions softly to her. In a moment I heard her activity herding them through. Then there was a kind of flurry and I sensed her running out further along the road towards the shoulder, and bringing back sheep that had scattered in that direction – all this mere sounds without sight, confused conjectures and surmises in my mind, until finally there was no more activity, but silence.

I closed the gate, hoping all the sheep were in, and went down to the house for a flashlight. In its light I picked up a few glints of wool from the field, but there was no question of counting sheep. Stub, lying not far from the gate, refused to move, even to follow me just as far as the house. I carried her into the kitchen. She refused to get up off her sack for a bowl of warm milk placed right in front of her or for solid food. For twenty-four hours Stub just lay there, unmoving, sometimes awake, sometimes sleeping. Finally (it was a relief to me) she got up, ate something, walked about. The day after that she was running again, eager for more work, to be working sheep.

There was a final irony. I learned later that prices mended just as we were leaving the mart. The fair had finally been exhausted, all sheep sold, and the merchants, some of whom had come from as far away as Belfast and Dublin, moved on to Donegal. Prices recovered dramatically. 'You would have sold your sheep, if you'd stayed,' I was told.

So the day had been a failure. But something had been gained: the new respect I felt for Stub and her ways of working.

Oddly enough it was while sitting in the house, on a rainy day perhaps, or in some interval in the day's work, or just after lunch, that I became aware of Stub's own learning, her self-teaching. I had a favourite armchair, a hard wooden chair like all the others in the kitchen, but with pleasant curving arms to support my own arms when I was reading. The chair stood not at the fire but next to the kitchen table, to be near the light, the window by day, the oil lamp at night. I had developed the habit of sitting in that chair with my right leg crossed over my left – invariably right over left, because the light was to my left, and without thinking I leaned my body towards it – and holding my book or magazine or paper, or whatever I was reading, as close to the window or the lamp as I could easily get it. While I was reading Stub would lie curled on her sack in the corner, a few yards from me, sleeping or dozing. From time to time she would stir, lift her head perhaps, or get up and stand for a minute, looking at me, or at nothing in particular, as though embarrassed, then paw the sack about and curl up on it again. I never correlated these stirrings of hers with my own thoughts until after another conversation with Peadar Nohar More about the ways of dogs.

It was apropos of dogs killing sheep. With the natural repugnance of anyone who hears about it for the first time I assumed that only a misbred dog could become a killer, through some fault in the blood, some accident in the genes.

'No,' Peadar told me emphatically. 'Your bad dog takes no great interest in sheep. It's the good dog that'll go to kill the sheep the quickest.'

As always when explaining some point of importance in farming, Peadar paused to let me assimilate his words; but it was a pause in which by look and attitude, by the sharp attention of his eyes upon me, he kept control of the conversation, allowed no interruption. As I opened my mouth to express surprise he immediately resumed.

'The dog will be always watching you. He'll know your ways. He'll know what's in your mind better than you know it yourself. And when you're not watching, that's the moment he'll slip off, and away.'

Peadar waved his right hand in a soft horizontal arc.

'That's when the harm'll be done.'

My own thinking was slow to readjust, my own mind slow to assimilate all that Peadar told me. Gradually, I did learn to notice that Stub's stirrings corresponded to some movement of my own. At first I must have thought that it was just the normal contagion of restlessness. Then I saw that, just as Peadar had told me, Stub was always alert, always watching me, even when she appeared to be sleeping the soundest. She seemed to be able to see through her closed eye-lids, or perhaps she had other means of sensing. I noticed that when I closed the book I was reading Stub would lift her eyelids ever so slightly. When I put the book down she would open her eyes all the way, become alert. Everything depended then on what I would do next. If I picked up the weekly newspaper and turned my attention to it Stub would at once settle back into her doze. If I looked around at my feet – indicating, I slowly realized, a change of footwear – she would sharpen her gaze.

Having got so far in my understanding of Stub's observations and deductions, it was easier to see the rest. If I was wearing my leather boots, heavy black leather from Czechoslovakia kept carefully waterproofed and used on walks to town or around the hill – if I was wearing those and started to unknot the laces and loosen them Stub would simply continue watching curiously. If I then reached for my old sandals she settled quietly back for a snooze. If I picked up my wellingtons though, and put my feet into them, then she would sit up, or stand up, and yawn perhaps, and get ready to go outside with me. She knew we would not go very far. Wellingtons are for dunging the byre, or doing some other (to Stub) not very interesting work around the yard, or not very far from it, activity for me but not for her; but at any rate it was a chance to get out of the house. The major signal for action was when I went from the sandals or wellingtons to the boots. The black leather boots were a real sign of activity, the kind Stub liked, a long walk perhaps, or at the least a visit to some neighbour, and possibly, what she preferred to everything else, work with the sheep, work on the hill with plenty of running and herding. The black boots brought her quickly to her feet. Once through the door she quickly began running out ahead of me and then back again, urging me on, almost challenging me, I thought, with eager leaps into the air in front of me, looking at me as she did so. The leaps seemed to say: 'Let's get on to the sheep.'

It was one of the times we were out on the back of the hill looking through the seventy bought-in ewe lambs. To begin with, there was a certain tension always in my mind connected with those lambs, because it was the first time we had ever tried buying in lambs and wintering them on the hill. The normal Blue Stacks procedure was just the opposite. Lambs were born on the hill in the spring and kept there with their mothers through the summer, but when autumn came they were either sold away or went to more sheltered, warmer grazing ground in the valley, nearer the sea. Buying in lambs and keeping them on the rough hill, often with little shelter from winter storms, was an innovation, and in the nature of an experiment. There was not only the danger that they would be weakened by and succumb to the wind and chill of the open hill, there was also the risk that they would simply decide to wander off, in search of better grazing, or just in an attempt to get back to the ground they were reared on, as sheep so often do. There were fences running along each side of the long strip of hill I had them on, but on one side, the side toward 'the wild hills' and Blue Stack, the fence was old, rusted in places, uncertain. A determined lamb could hunt around until she found a weak spot, a way through. I would have to hope none would. In my favour was the fact that that stretch of hill had been saved, had been free of sheep for several months, so that the heather and grass were able to recover, to grow out fresh and clean. The hospitality of the fresh grazing was meant to override the hostility of wind and weather.

Anxious about the results of this experiment, and constantly mindful of the money that had gone into buying the lambs, I started them on soft park land at first, until they got used to the place, the farm, and to seeing Stub and me walking around looking at them. After a few weeks on the fresh grass of the park I transferred them to the paddock on the hill. A fortnight there and then to the open hill. Since they had not been born on the farm, were not 'haunted' to it, I made a habit of going out on the hill every evening to count them and bring them together into a flock at a big landmark rock, a dolmen-like boulder on the crest, or sometimes, if storms seemed to be coming, to drive them over the crest from the back of the hill to the front, to be nearer to the house. It was the final task of the day for me, coming just before dark, and it was easy enough in September when the days were still long and nightfall did not come on too early, and even in October, but as the northern winter solstice approached dusk came earlier and earlier through November and December, a long, slow dusk, as gradual in its dim light as the slow sliding sunset of the bright summer days had been. It was a question of starting a few minutes earlier every afternoon, and sometimes that calculation of time was upset too by sudden hail-storms that we took shelter from on the lee side of overhanging ridges of deep turf, or by mist that shut off our view of anything that was more than a few yards from us. All these things added to the uncertainty I felt, and to my own inner tension when I went out to gather the lambs.

This particular day all those conflicting currents of thought and feeling were complicated, intensified, by outside concerns I brought with me to the hill. What was I so angry about, I wonder? Some minor detail of business, perhaps, some small matter not worth an hour's thought on a late fall or early winter's day, no doubt some petty annoyance with some local merchant who had gone back on his word, deceived me in some small, essentially insignificant way. (It is being deceived that annoys as much as any loss that goes with it.) Possibly it was something more remote, hence seeming more important, some dealings being carried on by mail, thus involving a hiatus of days between the sending of the carefully reasoned statement and the awaited reply. Whatever it was that engrossed my thoughts that evening, though I was going bodily to the hill my mind was elsewhere, and I was divided, abstracted, though not myself conscious of being so. My thoughts ran over my remote preoccupation while my feet carried me up the hill and my eyes looked for sheep. For Stub these regular late-afternoon climbs to the back of the hill had become the high point of the day, and she always responded with the same signs of enthusiasm: the eager tension of her body, the alertness of her eyes and look, her high challenging leaps into the air before me and facing me as we left the house and turned up the road towards the hill gate.

It was an afternoon of low clouds and intermittent showers of cold rain spitting from the west. Although there were no hail-stones the drops of rain themselves bounced back from the areas of ground where the turf was bare of grass, or from the occasional broad rocks, and as they fell slantingly against my cheek or forehead I felt them sting. I pulled the woollen hood of my duffle coat over my head and buttoned the top button, automatically leaning forward and into the wind as I did so.

Stub took little notice of the weather, eager as she was to get on to the back of the hill and to the sheep and the work that was her daily demonstration of loyalty to me. My attention was elsewhere as she ran ahead of me for fifty or sixty yards, then stopped and looked back and returned by a wide meandering arc to where I lagged behind, keeping to my foot for a time, all the while sniffing ground and air in investigations of things known only to herself. At intervals she would pause and face the wind, leaning her body into it, raising her nose and sniffing inquiringly. Her attitude as she did so suggested to me that she was identifying already known, familiar odours, gathering information on neighbours, or on their dogs, keeping track of the movement of a local fox or badger or hare, or locating sheep. Her progress up the hill, which so often seemed random to me, was a continual plotting out of the patterns of smell left on air and ground by other animals and men.

As we climbed my mood grew worse. The steep upward climb over rough ground intensifies every mood, good or bad. The heart beats heavier and the blood flows in stronger, fuller currents, and the body's inner weather responds accordingly. By very reason of my bad mood I had misjudged the time that afternoon, had waited a few minutes too long before slipping off my sandals and pulling on my black boots, and so was under additional pressure from the early dusk. Becoming aware of the failing light, I leaned into the hill and hurried my steps even more.

Once over the crest I wondered, as I did every evening, whether I could locate the sheep from above and so avoid the long downhill walk to the river, and the consequent exertion of

106

the returning climb. My eye ran over the deep heather and high rushes that dominated the surface of the hundred or so acres before me. Sheep, especially young sheep, are harder to find from the top of a rough hill, being more concealed by the vegetation, than from the bottom. I could count most of the lambs, but not all of them. As usual, I decided on a compromise: I would descend half way to the river and walk along the hill on a line parallel to both river and crest. Stub herself had not waited for a signal from me. Once over the crest she had swiftly moved away.

Whistling abstractedly for her to follow, I headed diagonally down the slope and towards the western fence, the climb, the weather, the oncoming darkness all constantly intensifying the unexpressed anger I was carrying with me that evening. As I found clumps of lambs grazing along the slope I turned my steps downward and around them in order to send them both uphill and towards other groups of lambs I had passed, gesturing without thought my visual signals to Stub to indicate how I wanted her help, where I wanted her to run. I assumed she was following my signals as I gave them, and so paused each time only as long as each gesture took, and then turned and continued on towards the western fence. In a few minutes I was there and reversed my direction, coming back eastwards along the hill, scanning with my eyes all the land above and below me as I went. The lambs moved on ahead of me, slowly merging from small groups into steadily larger ones. I looked ahead to the other end of my land and saw what I guessed to be all the rest of the lambs. As I was already bringing the lambs that were on my part of the slope in towards the centre, I expected Stub to do the same for those that were on her end, and I raised my hazel stick to indicate where I saw the other lambs, and called to Stub to go out. In the dim light Stub's dark body blended into the heather, itself growing dark with advancing evening, and it took a moment for my eyes to locate her by spotting the white fur of her neck and chest. I expected her to be leaping into the air, her head craned high, looking for signals from me, and it was only gradually that I noticed that, so far from jumping up, she seemed to be staying closer to the ground than ever. Then I saw that she was also hardly moving, not obeying my signals at all, shifting position only slightly as I walked towards the part of the hill she was on. I saw at last that she was paying no attention to the sheep at all, but kept her eyes steadily on me.

My anger, already seething against my unseen human antagonist, foamed over. I shouted a command. Stub moved back a few yards and stopped, slinking into the ground, but always observing me closely. Anger and indignation combined as I saw her fail to follow my directions. The next command contained the growled implications of a threat. Stub hardly moved. I changed my command, and called her to come in to my foot, turning and walking towards her at the same time. Stub backed off. Now it was at her that I was angry. So unreasoning had my emotions become that I followed her and tried to get hold of her. I was still unaware of the thoughts that were crowding my mind, sensing only vague preoccupations that I tried to hold within myself while actually attending to the gathering and counting of the lambs. I had no idea that my inner feelings were showing and could be read, certainly no suspicion that Stub could read them. Otherwise why had I worked out such an elaborate system of signs and gestures and whistled or shouted instructions? But if it was not the precise content of the thoughts she read, it was at any rate the most important part of them, the intent.

Completely unprepared for her behaviour then, it seemed to me an amazing and wilful disloyalty. The very fact that she was always such a loyal dog increased my annoyance. For a moment I paused, hesitated, knowing the futility of chasing the dog when she would not come. I leaned on my stick and let my gaze fall to the ground at my feet, the heather covered with drying, fading, bell-like pink blossoms, the coarse grass reddening in the fall chill, the tall rushes that grew up above my knees and brushed my thighs and even my waist. Vaguely, I became aware of the sound and movement of the bog-tinted water of the stream below me rushing out of the higher hills to the east. The rain spitting diagonally from behind me caught my cheek, my nose, and ran down along my jaw and chin. It was only for a few seconds that I stood that way. Then I lifted my gaze, looking into the distance at the hills, the mist, the uneven grey clouds that suddenly were very low, then back at Stub. Seeing her shrink away from me in fear, but still close to me, not moving off entirely for home and leaving me to cool my anger alone, I began to understand the reason why she was not working for me, would not come to me.

In that instant I realized that Stub would only come to me if I changed my very thoughts. The effort seemed enormous. Probably I had never tried to do such a thing. Probably I had always simply let my thoughts move in their own channel as they chose. My first attempt failed, did not fool Stub. If my voice and face changed their expression at all, as I at least thought they did, something still remained that made Stub keep her distance.

The message was clear. I made one more try to free my mind of anger – against anyone, anything – and in that instant it suddenly seemed to me as if my mind did become free, did empty itself of its distant burden, as though some inner counterpart of the dim evening's wind and rain and the rushing water of the stream had poured through me and carried away my oppresssive thoughts. Stub, still watching me intently, anxiously, her ears erect, her eyes fixed on my face, saw the change at once, and she raised her body from the low crouch she had kept all this time, lowering her erect ears and letting them fold back towards her head in sign of submission and reconciliation. She came to me, crouching again in the last few yards and settling on the ground a few feet from me on her stomach, her forepaws directly out in front of her. It was her silent sign of loyalty, of solidarity with me.

I was overwhelmed with admiration and affection. Bending my knees and squatting down, I held out my hands towards her. She came the remaining few feet and I began to stroke her head and the fur of her long back with my palms, speaking to her softly, affectionately as I did so. The words came from me spontaneously, words of sudden gratitude to Stub for what she had taught me.

'Oh my keen observer of footwear!' I said, 'my dear, sweet keen observer of footwear!'

So we gathered the lambs that night, but later on when I thought back over all this I wondered whether in the time we worked together I had made Stub a better dog or a worse one. It was a question that was in my mind a lot of the time those first years, the question I asked myself more and more about everyone I came into contact with there, about the men I worked and dealt with, each individually, the question I asked more and more about myself: whether we made those about us, animals as well as men, the earth itself and the land we worked, better or worse. For that is the test of a man.

THE WINDCHARGER

The idea of the windcharger went back to well before the fuel crisis. It was part of the aspiration to independence and self-reliance we brought with us to the farm. It was part of our personal revolt against the modern world in which we had for so long felt ourselves as purposeless, purely mechanical parts and pieces of a great machine that moved and in its motion rolled us around and along with it, with no apparent meaning we could detect, entirely uninfluenced by what we thought of as our own wills, our own opinions. To break out of that meaningless pattern of geared cog-wheels, to have an independent existence, seemed to us not merely freedom but self. It was to become your own self. Or at any rate to make a start in that direction, the first step of what would be a long exploration. For who in that massive city world that we had always known, whether in willing co-operation with its vast organisation or in futile resisting protest to it, could be certain that he knew anything about himself? And so we had no idea how long this journey of discovery might become.

From the first we were sure, almost obsessed with the idea, that we did not want the electric wires and poles of the Electricity Supply Board anywhere near our house or land. It was not merely that they marred the aesthetic appeal of an uninterrupted landscape. We were still too uncertain of our own instincts to be sure that the aesthetics of landscape had anything more profound about them than the compositional elements of line, colour and form we had heard museum lecturers talk about. Dimly, we sensed that there was something important about the sequence of high wooden poles that followed one another across the slopes and rounded hills, carrying and universally connected by the continuous grey double lines of insulated copper cable, one line, we knew, carrying the current to, the other carrying it away again from,

111

the farm houses they ultimately led to. There was something about the poles that made them seem like huge, brash crosses against the sky. Thinking about it, I wondered how the idea had entered my mind. The symbol was not appropriate.

These poles and lines that had brought ease and relief from toil to so many hard-pressed men and, even more, women could not be thought of as symbols of a crucifixion. The significant element was not the poles but the lines themselves, those endlessly interconnecting black lines that ran in undeviating parallel to the rolling earth beneath them, ceaselessly carrying power back and forth from some central source of energy out to all the separate scattered dwellings. It was not the poles but the wires that so perfectly expressed the change that had come over the countryside, the loss of just those qualities and elements we had come looking for. They expressed better than any other symbol we could have devised the transition from the narrow horizon of the men of the past, their intense relationship with their own earth beneath them and their own sky above them, to the modern men we ourselves were, divorced from the earth, devoid of a sense of its creative force working beneath us, our horizons as vast as the limits only of our radio and television sets, knowing more about events in Peking and Cape Town than about the lives of our own neighbours, possibly of our own families. We sensed the dilution of those ways of life that were once also expressions of life itself: local, practical, intensely human. It seemed to us that men had exchanged a vertical orientation, a way of seeing the world that, narrow as it was, could be at once both profound and elevated, for a horizontal one, oriented in all directions, endlessly broad, thinly shallow.

The reason, therefore, for wanting the windcharger was not quite practicality. Disguised as practicality, it was something else. It was the symbol and sense of independence, of being within ourselves, of using our own resources. For in the first arrogance of owning land we may have thought of even the air and the wind as our own.

There was far too much else to do – buildings to repair, roofs to thatch, fences to put up, ground to dig – to find time for putting in the windcharger. Instead, we struggled along with other primitive substitutes for electric light: candles first, then oil lamps that burned with a yellow flame and sooty wick,

112

then the pressure lamps that hissed and emitted a coarse white light more irritating than genuinely bright, and finally the long-glass-chimneyed silent lamps that seemed almost as good as electricity itself, so much better were they than what came before.

Occupied with other problems, or perhaps only caught in the inertia of easy habit, we put up with the many disadvantages and the inconvenience and the smell of the oil itself that arrived in two- or five-gallon plastic cans, and sloshed and slopped through the ill-fitting caps and slithered around and down the sides of the containers, then spilled again when being poured into the narrow-mouthed reservoirs of the lamps themselves. It was a tedious routine, especially in the middle months of the winter when the days were only eight hours long and the noonday sun never rose higher in its long, low curving glide across the sky than what seemed a few feet or yards above the distant southern horizon. The coming of spring with its impatiently awaited and then suddenly arrived lengthening out of the days brought tremendous relief from the task. In spite of all that, however, the windcharger itself was an even bigger task. To find one, buy it, ship it and erect it were huge efforts in a land so short of employable labour, so poor in skills. What if we should make the effort and then find that the windcharger did not work after all?

So it was put off, and even the oil crisis did not bring us much closer to it. Though there was a lot of talk on the radio about alternative sources of energy, and especially about windchargers, frequent postal inquiries brought little practical information in return. We had almost forgotten about the windcharger and were pondering the possibility of installing a three-hundred-gallon oil reservoir tank – a twelve-year supply, but one that the neighbours would help us use up when theirs began to fail, as it always did in the weeks around Christmas – but the mere cost and incongruity of the empty tank brought us back to the windcharger again. The oil tank, after all, was only another form of dependence on the outside world.

It was by chance, however, that we actually heard about an available windcharger, a working one, that was up for sale. Partly by chance, because in a sense it was the tarring of the road that led to the windcharger. If the county had never tarred the road we would not have got to know John Fetey. John was

113

the man who made the road. I say 'made' the road, but of course I am using the word loosely. John was the 'ganger' – what I would call the foreman. I suppose it would really be the county engineer who is entitled to official credit for making the road, though his round soft girth suggested that he spent more of his time at business luncheons and official banquets than out making anything material. Or perhaps the assistant county engineer laid claim to the road, because he did actually drive out every week or so to where the work was going on to inspect the road-crew's progress. The regional works supervisor was far too modest to lay claim to any distinction. And, after all, it was the men themselves who made the road – because the road was made, not machined: the stones were cracked with heavy hand-swung sledges, the gravel spread and filled by ordinary man-wielded shovels, and the draining and levelling and spreading of the fine cracked limestone surface was all done by the men, by hand. Only the spraying on of the tar and the final rolling were machine work.

But I say John made the road because that was true. In spite of the occasional visits of the assistant county engineer or the regional works supervisor, it was John who worked everything out. He sampled the various gravel pits looking for suitable stone, he sounded the old bog road to discover how far down he would have to go to find something solid, he determined the grading and in some cases even the course of the road, and as he was dealing with all those problems of planning he was also swinging the sledge along with the men, or the shovel, or whatever tool was going. He did most of the engineers' work for them and about as much of the physical work as any of the crew. Finally, he practised the diplomacy necessary to placate local householders who themselves had so loudly demanded the improvement and tarring of their road, but then grew irate at the delays and inconveniences caused them while the road was being made.

It was through the making of the road that we got to know John. One night we decided to go rambling to his place. He was sitting relaxing in his kitchen by the fire when we came in, with three or four of his children around him and his wife across from him at some needlework that she put aside from time to time to see to some baking she had in the oven. She was as full as he was lean, for he was as hard and lean as the roads he made, she as soft as the rounded loaves and cakes that were always going into or coming out of the range. Since John was a ganger it surprised us to see shelves full of books in the room, things like encyclopaedias of world knowledge and sets of history. That was another side of the ganger.

The windcharger came up just before we left. It was all part of what turned out to be a long misunderstanding. When we mentioned our idea of looking for a windcharger, John's wife told us that she knew where there was one for sale. We must have pricked up our ears at once, for she quickly added that it may already have been sold. At any rate, she knew that someone else was also interested in it.

It was clear that having mentioned the windcharger she then suddenly felt she might have been doing the wrong thing by bringing potential competitors in to bid against those other friends of hers and John's. Then, after a moment's hesitation, she decided that they would either have taken or rejected it by then and that she could safely tell us who owned it, where he lived and when to find him at home.

Conny Willy Bann, the owner of the windcharger, also worked the county roads. He drove one of the big council trucks that carried gravel to the construction sites. John knew his schedule and told us that if we were at his house by five o'clock exactly we would be sure to find him home. He knew that because, he said, Conny quit work exactly at five every evening. For a moment I was puzzled, then I remembered that on the county road-crew quitting time was really quitting time less travel time home. So when the crew was working on a remote road like ours somewhere in the hills, they quit a good deal earlier than when they were working in closer to their homes.

While that sounds like cutting corners on rate payers' money, all those men on the road crews were farmers too. They had sheep and cattle at home to see to, to fodder and milk, and in the spring they had to get their crop of spuds into the ground, in summer to mow and win their hay, their corn in autumn; and in winter the days were almost too short and the nights too early for any work around the farm and it was hard enough to do the minimum – all that work after hours, after their regular day of hard labour with picks and sledges and shovels. So the early leaving was not strange. On the contrary, there was something reassuring about Conny Willy Bann's punctuality. It implied that he kept things tidy.

John did not know where Conny had found the wind-charger – 'somewhere in the North,' he thought – but he told us that Conny had installed it himself and always serviced it himself. That increased our interest, because installation of the device was a major problem, where to put it to catch the wind best, how to construct whatever tower or scaffold it would need, the wiring of the house, and so on. When we left John and his wife that night and started home we were almost convinced that we would be the buyers of the windcharger. On the other hand, we wondered if someone else had not been smart enough to get it first. John's wife remarked, however, that she was pretty sure their friends had decided against it.

The next afternoon we left our place a little before five o'clock. It was only a twenty-minute drive to Meenafad, the townland where Conny Willy Bann lived, and obviously there was no point in being there just at the moment he arrived home from his day's work. It would be as well to give him time to have his cup of tea. We followed John's directions easily. Every turning and every signpost was exactly where he said it would be, the distances and landmarks he gave us were utterly precise, reminding me that I had heard it said that he had worked on almost every road in the county, and knew the whole system as well as he did his own farmyard. We turned off on to a tiny side road that was little more than a lane. At first I thought it incongruous that a road so narrow and obviously unimportant should be as well-tarred as that one was. Its surface was equal to any I had seen in the county. Then I realized that that was a confirmation of the fact that we really were on the right road to the house of a long-time member of the road-crew.

We turned into the first lane, and came to a neat white farmhouse with a few whitewashed stone outbuildings laid out in such a way as to enclose a farmyard. As there were no signs of life I got out of the car and tried the kitchen door, but it was locked. I went back to the car and we went on, but the road deteriorated after that and began turning into a rutted gravel track, so we pulled up at the next house and got out to ask directions. A pleasant old lady told us we had come too far. We were in Meenafad, but Conny Willy Bann did not live in Meenafad at all. His townland was Drimbui. But she was not sure anyone would be at home.

As I turned the car on the slippery dung-covered flagstones of the farmhouse yard I glanced at my watch. It was five-thirty, and Conny Willy Bann should certainly be at home. Then, thinking of what the old lady had said, I recalled the precise tone with which John Fetey had said we would be sure to find him when he got home at 'exactly five o'clock.' It meant, I realized, that after five o'clock Conny would be somewhere else, and suddenly I felt sure we would not find him at home that day.

The first problem, though, was to find the house. A few hundred yards back along the road we came alongside a woman. She had not been on the road when we had passed there only a few minutes before, and must have come out of one of the fields. Her manner of dressing suggested as much and was appropriate to the coldness of the weather that spring, for she seemed to be entirely covered, except her face, in windproof, rainproof clothing, sturdy boots almost like a man's, trousers, windbreaker, and a hood that covered the woollen kerchief around her head.

I stopped the car beside her, and she turned to look at us. Her mouth opened, suggesting the words 'Can I help you?' but she did not actually say them, or anything else, but simply stood looking at us in that attitude, her face alone expressing the question. The meaning was plain enough even without the words. At the same time, the failure actually to say the words clearly expressed her hesitation, her doubt of strangers and their intent.

'Hello,' I said, for she was on my side of the car, 'could you tell me where Conny Willy Bann lives?'

She looked at me blankly, then at both of us. For a moment it seemed as if we were nowhere near our goal. Wherever Conny Willy Bann lived, it seemed it was not on that road at all. At least, that is what her look seemed to say.

'Who?' she asked emphatically.

'Conny Willy Bann,' I repeated, though I thought I had spoken the name pretty clearly the first time. Perhaps all that clothing around her head made it hard for her to hear me.

The look became blanker still. Then I saw that it was something more than blankness. There was an element of questioning in it, and that too was meant to be hidden.

117

Altogether it was a poor attempt at a poker face, for it so clearly revealed that it was trying to hide its doubt, suspicion, mistrust. But it was not a hostile mistrust, just a questioning one. 'Who are these people?' it seemed to say, 'and what do they want with Conny?'

When I had seen that much in her face I realized that we had found the house at last. All that was needed was a password, a reassurance.

'We've heard he has a windcharger he wants to sell,' I said.

Her expression changed. Relief replaced suspicion. She became agreeable, almost smiled.

'Sure, I'm his wife,' she said. 'Come on into the house.' She gestured towards the house we had passed earlier, the tidy, modest white house only forty yards or so up a sloping lane above the road, and she led the way on foot up the gravel lane. We drove on behind her. I noticed that to open the front door that I had thought locked, she pulled it towards her first, using all her weight, and then pressed the latch down easily with her thumb and the door opened. She led us into her kitchen.

She was not a large woman. She was something under middle size, and when she sat down on a plain wooden chair next to the iron range she sat well forward on the chair so that her feet would reach the floor. When she had loosened her weather-proof jacket and put back the hood we could see that she had a round face, plump, like her hands, which were small and round, with short, plump fingers. She was a plain woman, still young and yet not young, and with that trace of anxiety that is in the face of almost every farm woman I had known in Donegal, in the face of all but the strongest and most vigorous.

She was trying to identify us, place us among the people she knew of or had heard of, so that she could picture our farm and our place in her mind. We were obviously foreigners, but living in that region, and on a remote farm, remote from the wires, or we would not have been interested in the windcharger. The Electricity Supply Board had brought electricity to almost every farm in the area so we should have stood out in her mind as among the few that still did not have it.

The name of our townland meant nothing to her, and she gave us a puzzled look that differentiated her in my mind from her husband, whom we had not seen or met, or from any man in that region, for the men all knew all the townlands by name

118

and usually by sight. Most of them had spent some time in almost every townland back in those pre-dole days when county road work was the only way of gettting a few pounds a week of steady income.

Since she did not know the townland, I mentioned the name of the farmer we had bought our place from. He too would be known to any local farmer, for he was a friendly, sociable man, a great talker and fond of pubs, and the remoteness of his land and house from the nearest one, or from any town, was almost proverbial. Again she had not heard the name. It was clear that identification was going to be difficult. Then suddenly her face brightened, and she realized that we were 'the two that bought the place in the hills.' We assented eagerly, with relief.

Conny himself was away to Donegal Town, she told us then. He would be back soon, she added. Then it turned out that that meant two or three hours, maybe more. If we wanted to go into the town we might be able to find him by the brown car he drove. She was not sure of the registration number. She had never really taken note of it.

Once she had identified us the talk turned to farming. She wanted to know what stock we kept, sheep or cattle or both, and what kinds and how many. How were they doing for us? It was mid-April and the lambing season had just begun, and so she started to talk about that. From where I sat I could look through a window in the back wall of the house with a long view of a gently sloping hill, a gradual but broad and extended slope of bare, unsheltered land, with no tree or shoulder to break the strong breeze that was sweeping the heather and coarse grass, and stirring the ends of the fleece of the blackface mountain ewes that were grazing at scattered intervals all across the long slope.

She started to talk about the lambing, and we could see that most of the responsibility for the sheep was hers. Of course that would have to be so with Conny away working on the roads five days a week. The good condition of the buildings and farmyard also indicated that he did a lot of work around the house. Someone would have to see to the animals.

It was lambing time and that was what occupied her most. As she talked I sensed that though she was talking about herself she was also watching us to see what our responses would be. That way, I thought, she could learn about us without having to ask too many direct questions. On the matter of the lambs, she declared at once that she had not had such bad luck that year. They were doing pretty well.

'We've only lost two for so far,' she added.

Two. Two lambs lost at the very beginning of the lambing. It seemed like an enormous loss to me, to have spent at least a year raising a ewe-lamb into a breeding ewe, another year waiting for her to lamb, and then in one of the three or four productive years of her life to have lost the lamb. It meant having kept that sheep for two whole years and having nothing for it.

But she obviously felt that to have lost only two thus far was fairly good going. It reminded me suddenly of the way things were on a hill farm. I say *reminded* me, for we had spent the winter keeping dry sheep, ewe-lambs in their first year that were busy growing into adult sheep and had nothing yet to do with breeding, with the intention of selling them again when they reached breeding age, and so we had not experienced that year the ravages in the population of new-born or young lambs that hit all the farms about us every spring, that had hit us in years past: foxes that carried off the new-born lambs, crows that pecked out their eyes, floods that carried them away, unseasonably late snow and frost that killed them with pains, the dull heat and barren east wind that withered the grass and dried up the ewe's milk - not to count the lambs born dead or the ewes that died in lambing.

'Only two for so far,' she had said, and then she went on to tell us proudly of the lamb she had saved that same morning. It was pure good luck that she had gone outside to have a look about. She did not know what had come into her head to take her out of the house at just that moment, for she had been baking, but she had gone out, and just as she got to the burn, which was in flood, she saw the lamb. It was one born only a few days earlier, a fine big ewe-lamb – she knew it at once by the white star on its face – and as she caught sight of it it was rolling over and over in the flood and being swept away down the stream. She had got there, by some good luck, just in time, for in another minute the lamb would have been out of sight down the stream and they would never know what had happened to it. She was just able to rush into the burn and get hold of it and drag it out.

120

'I thought he was drownded,' she said.

She took the lamb straight into the kitchen, herself half soaked, and wrapped it in woollen cloths and rags and put it beside the warm range where the loaves were baking, and hoped it would revive. Then she saw that it was still breathing, just a little, and she got it to drink some methylated spirit from a dosing bottle and then a little warm tea with milk and sugar. Gradually, it had revived and in the late afternoon she had put it out again with its mother. We could see how obviously proud she felt of her good fortune and of the good nursing that had enabled her to save the lamb. All in all, though, it reminded me again of the unequal struggle between the hill farmer and his farm.

Then she told us, too, about times Conny had found sheep ailing on the hill and had gone up with a creel and carried them down in it and tried to cure them, or put them in the boot of the car, the standard Morris Minor of the small farm, and rushed them to the vet. It seldom did any good, she said. Sometimes they were dead before he was even on the main road.

She was glad to have someone to chat with, and wanted to talk. At the same time, she had to be reserved about herself and not give out too much information to strangers. A certain amount, of course, would bring a response from us and so she would learn something about us in return and could then bring the talk back to the windcharger we had come to see. There seemed to be a three-way conflict going on inside her: to talk about herself, and not to talk about herself, and to remember that she should be trying to sell us the windcharger and so be doing something practical that would please her husband when he got home – like saving the lamb.

Talk about sheep turned out in a sense to be a dead end, for we had nothing very interesting to report about our own sheep. Because they were all young and not breeding-sheep they had all come through the winter relatively easily, and then, at just that moment in early spring when the breeding ewes were heaviest in lamb and beginning to go down under the strain of the long winter, the bitter weather and the cold, wet winds of spring, the dry sheep began to 'mend', to improve in condition on the little bits of grass that were beginning to grow and with the lengthening of the days and the extra daylight that allowed them to graze for longer and longer each day.

While we talked she had been making tea and slicing bread, and when four young children appeared from another room where, we heard, they had been watching television, she already had the kitchen table ready with cups and plates, bread, butter, jam, milk and sugar. She poured the tea and the children ate and drank in silence, watching us but not interrupting the conversation, which by then was only chat, casual remarks made only to make some sound and avoid silence. Then when the children had finished their tea and gone back to the television set in the other room she yielded again to the temptation to talk about herself and her own farm and family and her life. On that particular day, a blowy, wet, chill afternoon, she was preoccupied about her oldest child, a healthy little girl of about eight or nine, with bright black eyes and black hair, who looked full and round and strong to us. Evidently she had not always been so, and soon we were listening to an account of an illness that had occurred some years before, when the girl was only two or three years old, and was found choking in her bed one winter night, barely able to breathe.

It was a Sunday night and doctors were hard to find. In the old Morris Minor mother and father had rushed the child from one doctor's house to another, a little the way, perhaps, they sometimes rushed a sick sheep to the vet, possibly a little despairing too, as they usually were with the sheep, then finally to a small hospital some thirty miles away. She remembered the child's black hair plastered down to the small head with sweat, the heat from the small body, and the struggle for breath. It was both an attack of asthma and something worse. Even in the hospital Sunday prevailed and there was no doctor to be found. A sister had come and hastily taken the child's temperature and found it perfectly normal.

Then a regular nurse had been found, the temperature taken again, the fever identified, a doctor called and action taken at last. But what she remembered was the 'wee black head' and the weary child eagerly closing her eyes and seeking sleep and rest as the injection began to take effect and she could breathe again.

'I thought she would cry when we went to leave her in the hospital,' she commented finally, 'but she never did. *Leave me now to rest in my wee bed,* she seemed to be saying, she was that weary.'

While she talked we had been drinking the tea she had poured and eating the bread and butter she had put before us and so we had no need to interrupt her with pointless remarks. A nod or a grunt was sufficient indication of our attention and affirmation that we were listening. She was glad enough to talk without interruption, talk that reflected so well the loneliness and the hard touch-and-go life on a hill farm where, alone most of the time, she could never be sure what crisis would come, what special action would be needed to save a lamb, a child, a husband's affection.

We finished our tea and moved back from the table. She sighed as she cleared away the dishes and then folded her hands together as she sat down again on the edge of the wooden chair by the range. It was clear then that we were about to talk about the windcharger.

It was, she said, a very good one and had never failed them. Conny had installed it himself and had always serviced it himself. They had got all their light from it for several years. When the Electricity Supply Board came around canvassing they had decided to 'go in with the others' – with their neighbours.

She looked at us doubtfully at that point, and then explained that if one family stood out and refused the electricity from the Electricity Supply Board the installation charges would be a lot higher for the remaining families. The doubtful look indicated that she knew the motive was not a usual one in Donegal farm communities, where neighbours generally find it hard to co-operate on anything longer term than the building of a hay stack – indeed, prefer to differ, if only for the sake of their individuality. To us, however, a switch from the windcharger with its many difficulties and its primitive, uncertain supply of power to the effortless, steady flow of the Electricity Supply Board generators seemed a natural move for a practical farmer. It was an obvious rise in the family's standard of living, and we hardly looked for any explanation of the change. We had heard stories of the trouble people had had with windchargers during the war when the shortage of lamp oil had driven ingenious men to construct their own. Lack of wind was not the only problem. Too much wind could also put the mechanism out of

123

order. Or the blades got stuck and would not turn or failed to swivel into the shifting wind. Batteries ran down or overcharged, and so on. Common complaints about windchargers. For the ordinary family the Electricity Supply Board was clearly a change for the better.

A strong gust of wind rushed across the bare hill behind the house and I remarked that they were in a good place for a windcharger, since there always seemed to be plenty of wind and little shelter to break its force. Again she looked at me doubtfully, and I was afraid that I had inadvertently cast some doubt on the ability of the windcharger to work well in a less bare and unsheltered place. Also, I thought, my remark may have suggested that her farm was not as pleasantly located as our own. She simply replied, again through her doubtful look, that indeed it had never failed them. Even after the Electricity Supply Board lines had been connected there had come stormy winter nights when the power was cut off because a wire was down or a transformer knocked out somewhere, or because everyone had cut their own supply at the fuse box for fear of lightning. Then theirs was the only house in the neighbourhood that had light. You could look out and see all the other houses in darkness, but their neighbours would look over and see their house with the light. While the other houses were without power, they could still be sitting watching the television.

Television? Had they run a television set on their windcharger? I was surprised at that. Unless they used a small set with a rechargeable battery or had a particularly sophisticated windcharger. I remembered John saying that Conny had found it 'somewhere about the North', and realized that it must be of a better make than most people in Donegal remembered from the war years. I had read about Swiss windchargers that could supply current at high voltages and run every kind of appliance.

So we sat and discussed the matter idly, the installation, the wiring and so on. There was little specific concerning the working of the machine itself that I could ask her, since it was Conny who attended to the whole thing. In spite of its convenience Conny had finally decided to sell it. Of course it was useful in a power cut, she added, but those times were not very often. Even so, it was no work to go out and get it started

124

when it was needed. One thing about it that was very good and worth mentioning: it was not at all sore on diesel.

We must have paused and looked at each other in surprise as we assimilated this new fact about our windcharger – by then we had both gone a long way towards thinking about it as ours.

'Does the windcharger work on diesel?' I asked.

'Yes,' she answered brightly, 'and that's not near as dear as petrol. You would be running it for such and a much a time, you see, and it would take such and a much of the diesel. Like your vehicle. Only it would be far less sore on the diesel than your car on the petrol. You would run it all night for a few pence.'

Then I saw my misunderstanding, the simple misunderstanding of a word. After five years in the Blue Stacks I still had not learned that the term *windcharger* was generic for all generators, diesel or otherwise. But we had been living in Donegal long enough to know that things often turned out to be something else from what they first appear or are supposed to be. If we had started out when we first lived there by talking about 'wild-goose-chases' we had long since given that up. Most chases were after wild geese, we had discovered. But we had also found that when we went looking for one thing we sometimes finished up by finding another, possibly better. So instead of asserting indignantly that we had come to see a windcharger, I changed my way of thinking as quickly as I could, and we went on to discuss the generator.

There was not much to discuss. She knew nothing about the way the machine worked, only the result, and she had already told us how good that was. We asked about the noise.

'Noise?'

'Doesn't it make noise when it's running?'

'I suppose it does,' she said. 'We never heard it.' Then, seeing my look, she added: 'Sure you can see it yourself if you come when Conny's here.'

She seemed to be calculating inwardly for a moment, and then continued: 'Can you come on Sunday at half two? He has his dinner at two o'clock on Sundays, and he's sure to be here at half two. Or make it three o'clock, that would be better. He'll just be finishing his tea.'

We settled on Sunday at three. She would not let him away, she said, even if we were a bit late. As long as they knew we were certainly coming he would surely wait for us.

As we drove out of the yard and down the lane she and the four children came out of the house to see us off and wave good-bye. As soon as we were on the road again we began to discuss the metamorphosis of our windcharger and to go into the pros and cons of buying a diesel generator instead. The greater reliability and the larger power capacity were for it, the noise and the ugly presence of the oil tank, with all its implications, against it. It would be a compromise at best, a kind of half independence only. When the supply of precious imported oil was short and demand was high, where would we stand on the oil company's long list of customers?

By Sunday, however, abandoning philosophic scruples, we had warmed to the idea, and we were careful to leave the house early enough to reach Conny Willy Bann's with time to spare. We got there at five to three, but as we drove up the lane something about the aspect of the farmyard that day, something we could not determine or define, told us that that day, too, was not auspicious. It is funny how things are communicated that way, without words, without gestures. We sensed, even in the inanimate objects, the shed doors, the gates, the house itself, that this time too we were unlikely to see the object of our coming, the power-source.

As she opened the door we saw at once that the surmise was right. For a moment she looked at us in surprise, as if she had not expected to see us. That was only for a second. It was not an attempt at evasion or deception but an involuntary reflex, for she said at once: 'Conny's away to the hill. He had sheep to see to and he couldn't wait.'

She stepped out of the house and stood before us. 'Some way he's not right minded to sell it just yet, and he had to go away to the hill to see about some sheep that are away up. He won't be back for a good while.'

There was no point in looking disappointed, but she may have seen disappointment in our faces anyway.

'Of course,' she went on, 'if we could get it started you could see it working. Would you know how to start it? Conny starts it, you see, I've never. The handle is here in the house, the handle you put it running with. If you knew how to turn it over you could see it running.'

She called to one of her children to fetch the handle, which turned out to be like an ordinary crank-handle for an old car, and then she led the way to a low stone shed behind the house. We followed her, the four children around us. I ducked my head to enter the tin-roofed shed, and saw that it was cluttered with tools that had been set down at random after use and were lying about then in disorder. The light from the low door was blocked by the cluster of children around and in the doorway and the only other light was from a tiny window in one wall. A dark amalgam of oil and grease and sawdust coated the floor and the low, narrow wooden workbench that stood under the small window. It was hard to distinguish anything at all characteristic about the workshop except its clutter, for hand-tools and machine-tools, wood-working tools and motor-maintenance tools were all mixed up together. It was not an unusual condition for a farm workshop in Donegal, nor was my own place exempt from it. I had also learned how hard it is to keep tools neat and tidy in cramped, dark quarters, with all the complicated problems involved in trying to do everything about the farm, or almost everything, for yourself.

She went to the far end of the shed and opened a door that was only a few feet high. It revealed an even smaller shed, and in the dim light that seeped through the shed we were in I could see that there was some kind of object in the smaller shed that she meant me to look at. I bent over and squinted towards it. At first I made out nothing but an irregular pedestal or pyramid. Then I saw that a base two or three feet high had been built up and the generator fixed on top of it. As I stood awkwardly bent over waiting for my vision to adjust to the darkness, peering blindly into the little, low enclosure, the thought went through my mind that I had come face to face at last with the power-source.

It was a small, round, green machine gleaming with dark grease and oil. I looked at it for a moment and then peered more intently, hoping to make out something more. But that was all I could see, something green and small and metallic, round and gleaming with dark oil and grease. I stared at it insistently, silently asking it whether it generated a good supply of power, whether it ran reliably when it did run, and how much noise it made, and as I did so I felt the absurdity of letting such questions form themselves even involuntarily in my mind. Though I hoped my eyes would adjust to the darkness of the tiny sanctuary the machine was housed in, it became even darker as the children crowded around me and we blocked the small amount of light that could trickle through the tool-shed. There was nothing to be made out, really, nothing to be learned from standing there, bent over, peering in the darkness at this mute, greasy green lump.

I went out again into the wholesome daylight. As there was no point in conversation we went back to the car. It must have been plain that my humour was worn thin, though I tried not to show it. As we sat in the car and I prepared to turn the key she came over to us, her children following in silent curiosity.

'I'm sorry Conny's not here,' she said, 'but he had to go off to see about the sheep. This would be the only time he has, you know.' She paused, then explained. 'I suppose he's not right minded to sell yet.'

I mumbled some sort of assent. The matter seemed definitely settled, and at first I could not think of anything more to say. Then a sudden return of good humour prompted me. 'Sure,' I said, 'it'll be useful to you yet. He's right to keep it. You never know when you'll get a power cut.'

She looked at me doubtfully again. 'There are lots of people after it, you see,' she resumed. 'All kinds of people have come looking for it, and wanted it. They're terrible hard to find.'

She hesitated just for a second, watching us, and then went on. 'You don't know how much you'd want to pay for it? Conny could get it running, you see, and you could come back another time and see it.'

'Sure,' I said. 'Conny's wise to keep it. It could be valuable to you in years to come.'

But the conversation was not finished. 'If you knew what it would be worth to you, Conny could put it going another time and you could see how it works,' she said. 'They're terrible hard to find now.'

'I know they are,' I said. 'Conny's right to keep it.' I paused, getting together more good humour. 'Thanks a lot for your trouble,' I said. 'And best of luck.'

'Good luck,' she said and stood away from the car as I turned the key. We drove down the gravel lane and turned back on to the finely paved county road, moving at an easy pace through the bare hill landscape covered with heather and long, coarse red grass, with sheep grazing at intervals across the low slopes. It was a half sunny, half cloudy day, a kind of Donegal day when the landscape lies before you in stripes and patches of intense light and dark, brilliant light strips of luminously clear sunlight, chilly blue areas of dark shade. The contrast enhanced the beauty of the landscape, and as the shadows shifted rapidly across the fields and slopes near us and the distant hills, and the brilliant sun highlighted first one area and then another, a valley, a slope, the peak of a rounded hill, we commented to each other in short exclamations on the beauty of the country before us, forgetting as we did so our disappointment about the windcharger, forgetting even to discuss or mention it.

TWO LIVES

Things I do that Peadar Nohar More has never done:
   wake up to an alarm clock
   draw water from a tap
   brush my teeth
   write a letter
   read a letter
   wear a tie
   talk over the phone
   fill out a questionnaire
   pay taxes
   pack my bags
   catch a bus, train, plane
   drive a car
   drink coffee
   catch the flu
   sign my name.
Things Peadar Nohar More and I have both done:
   walk
   talk
   smoke
   drink tea
   go rambling
   sow cabbage, onions, carrots
   set spuds; dig them
   dip sheep, dose and shear them
   mow hay, oats, rushes
   milk the cow
   dung the byre
   train dogs
   go to the hill
   put up sheep-wire
   cut drains
   cut and win turf

thatch
make bread
do our own laundry.
Things Peadar Nohar More does that I have never done:
talk Irish
kill foxes with a stick; badgers, mink
save old sheep-dip against maggots
predict the weather by watching animals
never feel the cold
castrate lambs
bless himself after a meal
know old cures (curing a cow of a founder with bruised
    potatoes in a sack; curing her of the moozles by feeding
    her the soup of a fat hen; curing himself of a bad back with
    a weed poultice; curing an injured ankle with a prayer)
know old legends
know the special powers of priests
live in a house five hundred yards from the road
deduce prehistory
retell the Bible in another version (the wren and the robin go
    out from the Ark; midges stop the building of the tower
    of Babel; the Fire precedes the Flood)
see waterhorses, neels, dorhos
plait Brigid crosses
bring in Brigid
ponder the mysteries.

It was the evening before I left for America that these contrasts between Peadar Nohar More and myself came into mind. I had not been home for eleven years, so completely had I become absorbed in my new life in the hills, and the decision to visit the United States at last was made with some hesitation. I was, after all, at home, in another sense, in the hills.

At eight o'clock on the night before we were to leave, Peadar walked in the door. He had come to see us off. I thought at first it was just one of his usual visits, and that it just happened to coincide with the eve of our trip, because he said nothing to indicate that it was a special visit. It was only as he stayed later and later, filling pipe after pipe, that I slowly realized that he was giving us the traditional send-off for emigrants, sitting up with them through the entire night before their departure and

131

smoking and drinking and talking – and no doubt at other times singing and dancing – in a final long evening together before a leave-taking that might mean twenty years of absence, or longer, even a lifetime. Peadar was the last one faithful to this old tradition, as to so many, although he knew we were going by plane in five hours from Shannon to New York and not by slow immigrant ship, and that we would be back in weeks, not decades. It was my original puzzlement at Peadar's staying so late on the very night that I wanted to get to bed early, to be ready for the early start in the morning, that set my mind to considering the differences between us.

Once at home in America I was dazzled for three days and nights by the size and brilliance of New York and thought of nothing else, but on the fourth night, out in the New England countryside again, I lay awake until dawn and thought of my two homes, my two countries. I thought of Peadar's send-off, and then of other times we had spent together, working, rambling, talking, so that our lives and minds and tongues, so disparate at first (so disparate at our first meetings that neither could understand the other, or only barely when we spoke), gradually overlapped. It was then, away from the hills, that I began to sort out the ways I had that Peadar never would share, and the ways we were or had become (mostly through my learning from him) alike, and finally the things about Peadar that I could never learn or imitate, ways that belonged only to him and his own world.

If there were certain things that I did, like waking up to an alarm clock or drawing water from a tap, that Peadar never did, what did he do instead? He woke up to the rooster's call (for the hands of his old clock, which stood in a niche by the hearth where it would be dry, had not moved for a long while, and I doubt whether Peadar had ever known how to read the time or set the alarm), and he drew his water in a bucket from the burn that poured and fell from rock to rock down the hill beside the gable of the house; instead of letters he sent word with a friend, and got back word of mouth; instead of reading anything he listened attentively while others read or spoke, and remembered what he heard; instead of a tie he just buttoned his shirt and was done; he never travelled but simply stayed at home; and when he did go calling he went on foot or rode with others (but never has been more than a day's walk distant from the place where he was born, and where he still lives); drinks tea, stout, beer, whiskey, brandy, anything but coffee; stays well; lets others sign for him.

But of the things we have in common, some were common to both of us before I ever came to Meenaguse, things that most people do, or all people, like walking and talking and smoking, or drinking tea (though I prefer coffee), but more of them were things I only started doing after I settled in the Blue Stacks, things I learned to do there, often from Peadar: shearing sheep, dipping and dosing them; mowing grass for hay and oats for fodder, rushes for thatch; milking the cow (which Hannah Thomas, Peadar's neighbour across the river-valley on the slope facing his, taught me, striding over the hill one thunderstormy August day, because she had heard that I had bought a cow, and surmised that I would require teaching); dunging out the byre, training my dogs, putting up sheep-wire fences; cutting and spreading turf on breezy April days and gathering and thatching it in June when it was dry; cutting drains with a spade to carry off the water from wet places on the land; going to the hill almost every day to have a look at the sheep, or wandering into the high hills far from the house with one of the dogs to search for some sheep that had strayed; making bread when my wife was away, and doing my own laundry at those times too.

But, oddly perhaps, what draws Peadar and me most closely together are the things Peadar does that I have never done, will never do, even the little things, like the way he crosses himself rapidly after he has eaten, or plaits Brigid crosses from green rushes at the beginning of February and brings them into the houses of his neighbours (a plaited cross for every house), saying a prayer in Irish as he does so, in our case having first stopped in to teach us, every year anew, the Irish words with which we must respond and welcome the cross, welcome Brigid, and instructing us to be on our knees, so that the ceremony may be propitious; predicting the weather, some-times for only hours or days ahead, sometimes for weeks or months, by observing animals: dogs, sheep, hens, ducks, cats, badgers, birds, foxes; and the bigger things, like living in a house five hundred yards from the road, carrying in all supplies on his back, or under his arm, as his father and mother did too and however many generations there were before them in that same house and place (except that I have heard that they often carried entire hundred-weights of flour or meal not just from the road but the eight miles of distance and nine hundred feet of altitude from the town); and never feeling the cold, even on the first day of the new year, when I tramped through the snow to pay him a call and found the kitchen door open to the hill breeze and the snow at dusk; or the foxes and badgers he has killed, coming upon them alone at night and breaking their legs with his stick to immobilize them, then their skulls, or going after them by day with his dogs; or the stray mink he pursued and killed as it crept through the hollow spaces in an old dry-stone wall, tearing out the stones with his hands in the pursuit, cornering it finally and killing it, hanging it then in the roofless walls of an old byre as a trophy of his anger for the hens it had killed; and most important perhaps, the one thing that should divide us but actually draws us closer together, the difference in the language, the fact that Peadar speaks Irish; for, speaking Irish, the pure Irish of the hills learned not in any school but around the hearth and on the slopes of the remote hill farm, from parents who themselves learned it the same way, and so on through the generations, he also bore in mind and memory (and gradually I came to see that these things are always in Peadar's thoughts, are his constant silent companions) the old unwritten lore, the legends of the three men whose being alive now makes the continued existence of the earth and the lives of the rest of us possible (he himself knows one of them, he told me once, but stopped himself there and gave me no further information, sensing that he was profaning this knowledge never meant to be transmitted outside his native tongue), or his belief that the Flood was preceded by the Fire (what fire? I wondered, when he first brought the subject up), because throughout the deep layers of turf that cover the hills are found, buried to depths of eight or ten feet, the trunks of old trees impregnated with the bog itself and looking as if they had been charred by fire; and other stories that seemed to me Biblical but strangely transformed, much as the bog had transformed the appearance of the wood so long buried in it: the wren that was sent out from the Ark first, never to return, and the robin then, to return with a twig of fir; or the two men who decided to build a tower to heaven, and would have reached heaven too but that a swarm of stinging midges, the

134

first midges ever seen, came on them and put an end to their work; and along with the legends the things he himself had seen high in the hills and in the hill lakes and curraghs, the lake-dwelling waterhorses, the long-bodied winged eels, the sword-nosed dorhos; all of these and those other unseen, unspoken – at least to me, or to anyone who knew no Irish – mysteries of which I caught only glimpses, but which I knew Peadar lived by, had constantly in mind, pondering them.

Lying awake on a winter night in New England, four days home in America after eleven years away, thinking about all these things, it was one of the last nights of rambling together that stuck in my mind, that somehow embodied the meaning of our friendship.

'We must go down to Michael's one night,' Peadar said.

About once a year he and I rambled to the farm Michael and Peggy had bought several miles down the valley on the lower land to the south of us, selling the hill farm and its house to me a few years later. In the days when they were still in it the kitchen had been a nightly gathering place for neighbours on all sides. Their leaving also left an emptiness our coming could not fill. Too new to the hills, we did not even own a deck of cards, and it did not come into our heads to buy one and to pull out the kitchen table when neighbours came in at night, and put the chairs around it and set out the cards and be prepared to sit up and talk and drink tea or, on special nights, stout or beer or whiskey, until well into the morning. Had we done those things the pattern of nightly visitors might have re-established itself; but we had brought with us foreign ideas of the early-hours pattern of the farming schedule, and it took years for us to readjust to the long twilights and slow sunsets and sunrises of Donegal, the days that do not begin at first light but only hours later, the nights that stretch on, in summer, almost long enough to meet the following day. So neighbours came to us to talk for a while, but never for the all-night sessions of Michael and Peggy's time.

At first Peadar and I used to walk down to Michael's a few times every winter. As time went on that grew rarer as I became less adventurous. A few soakings when I got caught in sudden heavy Donegal showers on the long walks home probably influenced my point of view, and as Peadar grew older the distance from his house to ours and then down to Michael's

and back up again at the end of the visit became correspond-
ingly longer for his ageing legs. After a while our visits reduced
themselves to a single annual one, usually deep into the winter.
It was up to Peadar to decide when, and I never knew until the
time he stepped in the front door and sat down and we had
chatted for a while and he said, 'I had a mind to go down to
Michael's' in a way that was both suggestion and question, that
that was the night for the visit.

Before that we had always walked, sometimes on wet nights,
sheltering from the rain under the hoods of our duffle coats, or
stopping in at houses along the road and sitting by the hearth
until the shower was past or until the rain had softened slightly,
then going on; sometimes on winter nights when snow had
fallen and was still covering the fields and hills and roads, and a
bright moon made walking easy, almost like daylight, I
thought, enjoying the odd sensation of walking the unlighted
roads, their peaceful night darkness never interrupted by
lamps, without need for the flashlight in my pocket; striding
along side by side, unspokenly proud, both of us, of our
vigour, the ability to walk the hill roads at night, briskly,
without fatigue, without the fear of those shadowy beings that
kept some of our own neighbours in at night, gladly; proud too
of one another's company and admiration.

That was the main difference between all those other
rambles to Michael's and this one, for this time I had the old car
that I bought second-hand the summer before, and gradually,
try as we would to go against it, the car was used more and
more to get places, and walking less and less. Cautious, I
avoided all bad weather even with the car, heavy storms of
wind and rain, and above all snow and frost, deterred by the
narrowness of the hill roads and the steepness of the drop,
often, from the road down into the bog below, and the thought
of the soft emptiness of the bog, thinking that even if I landed
on four wheels I might not stay on them; but this night I had
agreed to take Peadar by car, and the slight hint of coming frost
could not put us off. We remembered times we had walked
glassy roads, never losing our balance on the smoothest of ice.
The night was dry and full of stars, the kind of night we would
have congratulated ourselves on having when we were on foot,
the kind of night when Peadar would look up for a while in
silence as we walked and then comment quietly, 'The stars

going wild with the frost.' This night I was unaware of all that, intent instead on the glowing green lights of the car dashboard and on the shifting images picked up by the headlights as we moved along.

As we reached Ardbahn we saw Jimmy Paddy in front of his house. I stopped the car and leaned over across Peadar to roll down the window on his side, the side Jimmy was on (for that was another thing Peadar never did, never touched any of the knobs on the door of the car, not knowing which was which, and having better manners than to fiddle around ignorantly, but let me turn or pull them for him), and Jimmy came over and leaned on the sill.

'We're going down to Michael's,' I said. 'Will you come along?'

'I will,' Jimmy said, 'but later. Go you ahead and I'll follow on. I have the cows to milk yet.'

'I could come back,' I said, 'and collect you. In about an hour?'

'Well. That might be all right too, but it's putting bother on you.'

'No. No bother. Only I'm going on a way to do a message before I go into Michael's. I'll leave Peadar off and go do my message, then if I'm done with that quick enough I'll be back for you again. If you're ready to leave before I get back, start on the road and if I'm coming up we'll meet.'

It was agreed, and Peadar and I drove on. I thought of the possibility of frost on the road later in the night. It was mid-January. The winter had been a mild, frostless one, but with the night so clear it was likely to freeze. At such times the road, criss-crossed with the overflowing water of the springs and the old, blocked drains, was hard enough to climb on foot, the more so at night when the frozen water was invisible, but could be even harder in a car. Still, we were already under way. I could not let my excessive caution turn us back.

I stopped at Michael's lane and let Peadar out. 'Tell them I'll be along in an hour,' I said, and watched him down the lane until all I could see was the glow of his flashlight moving in rhythm to his step. Then I drove on the four miles to Master O'Connaghan's, 'Master' because he was the master of a two-room schoolhouse, but the title, I thought, was appropriate for Brendan in other ways, for he had mastered so many of the useful crafts of Donegal life: carpentry, plumbing and house-construction generally (he and his pretty young wife, whose hands most times I visited them were continually busy producing white knitted bonnets, but who had put aside her knitting and taken up a shovel to help her husband mix and pour cement for their own house and then had taken a hand in putting the roof on the finished walls, herself cutting the rafters just because her own hands were more delicate than his, hence presumably more precise), but also boat-building and fishing; and, among it all, photography. That was what I wanted this night. I had a roll of film with me that I urgently wanted developed and printed. Looking back now, I find I cannot remember the reason for my haste, the urgency so uncharacteristic of life in the Blue Stacks, but I think it was all part of the new attitude that was one with the car itself, a machine-oriented attitude of movement and haste, one that was separating me from the harmony I had felt for so many years with the slow pace of the hill farm life around me.

In the event Brendan responded enthusiastically to my request, and after a quick supper we went up together to the dark-room he had constructed under the eaves. The smell of fresh spruce from the new rafters still filled the space. There as we chatted and the film went from tray to tray in the almost complete darkness, something in the situation and in our talk stimulated the perfectionism in both of us. After he had made the first contact prints of the newly developed film we began to discuss the best ways to print the individual exposures, and when the printing actually began we examined them with a more and more critical eye. I had thought the whole process would take only an hour or so, but I had forgotten that we would spend at least that long just talking and drinking tea – supper – before we even started on the film. Then had come the setting up of the equipment, the measuring and pouring of the chemicals, and so on, before the actual developing began. I had never been in a darkroom before and my impression of the speed with which things happened (an impression, I suppose, of instantaneousness) must have been based on movies I had seen when I was small, in which crucial newspaper photographs were shown first being snapped by the photographer, then an instant later becoming visible as the finished product in a darkroom tray.

I was so absorbed in the process that I did not notice time passing. Then I got carried away by having my own technician right there, only too willing to re-do any print that was not quite perfect. Brendan pointed out details I was unaware of, would never myself (used as I was to receiving back glossy little snapshots as the final result of my efforts) have noticed, and soon we were discussing contrast and size and fineness of grain. Other chemicals were poured and other papers were brought out from the dark drawers where they were carefully preserved from humidity and concealed from light, papers that would give more contrast, or less, or more detail, or a sharper effect or a softer one. I was intoxicated by this choice of possibilities never before experienced by me. Eventually, having amassed a pile of trial prints, we stopped for another cup of tea and found that Brendan's wife had gone to bed. Then we realized that it was after one o'clock. I thought briefly of Peadar at Michael's, pictured them wondering where I was, remembered too that I had said something to Jimmy Paddy about coming back for him, and then quickly dismissed that from my mind. I had become convinced that my roll of film demanded first-rate prints.

Brendan made the tea himself, and as we drank it and ate the bread and butter he put out to go with it our talk was all of photography, and especially darkroom techniques. Then he got up and went outside and I followed him. He had had a feeling while we were in the darkroom, he said, that there had been a hard frost. He turned out to be right, but he pointed out that there had also been a thaw and a second frost, showing me the little smooth mounds of ice that had formed, like frozen drops of water, all along the wind-shield and roof of my car. The roads would be slippery, he commented.

I ran my hand over the little mounds of frozen water on the car, and thought of the road. It would be slippery driving, I agreed, especially on the hills. Then I quickly forgot that too. The photographs seemed all-important.

We went back to the darkroom and became absorbed again in the work, trying different papers and different development times, and then getting interested in format and framing of the subjects, selecting parts of each negative to print and the right size to print it, and so on. Brendan must have been as intrigued by having a complete novice in the darkroom with him

139

expressing wonder at all the technical possibilities as I was by being there looking on. Time passed and we were engrossed. Then at a certain moment we were suddenly tired, both of us, and lost interest. The possibilities seemed to have been tried and there was no point in trying any more. Brendan remembered that he had to be up for school in the morning and I remembered Peadar and Jimmy at Michael's. We quit. It was four o'clock.

Outside, Brendan examined the frozen drops of ice again and decided that there had been yet another thaw and frost. The road would be very icy, he said.

'Watch yourself,' he added as I opened the car door to get in.

The car danced along the slippery narrow roads, but gently, as I drove gently, always regaining its grip on the smooth surface just as I thought it would slide into some hedge or ditch. I tried to remember the rules I had read for driving on icy surfaces, not using the brake, turning into the direction of the skid and so on, but when the car did begin to slip around there was no time to think about the rules and follow them. Whatever I did was automatic, without thought – like dancing – but it worked out all right. After a mile or two I began to feel I had the hang of it and that all would go well. In retrospect I can see that I must have been slightly intoxicated, not with drink but with the lateness of the hour and the newness of the night's experiences.

I pulled up at Michael's lane and hesitated as to whether I should risk disturbing him and Peggy, for I had decided that they were probably long since in bed and that Peadar and Jimmy had given up on waiting for me to come and had gone home on foot. Then I decided to go down the lane on foot to make sure. The house faced away from the road, with all the windows on the side away from me, so I could not tell if there was a light on in the kitchen or not. Walking down the lane, I noticed that extra quietness the night has as it verges towards morning, and I tried to walk more quietly myself so as not to disturb the silence and the sleeping world. I wondered whether I should not abandon the silly idea of going to the house and just go back to the car instead and home and bed.

As I rounded the gable of the house I saw that the lights were on in the kitchen, and I walked in without knocking, following the custom I had learned in the hills. Michael and Peggy and

Peadar and Jimmy were sitting on the wicker chairs in a little crescent, a kind of flattened semi-circle, facing the fire. They turned around when I came in and greeted me much as they would had I come in rambling at a normal hour of the night, and not at four-thirty in the morning. Peggy got up and moved another chair into place for me in the crescent near the fire. As they resumed their conversation I could tell at once that they did not mind or regret the lateness of the hour. On the contrary, their talk and laughter was as lively as I had ever heard it, and soon I realized that they were enjoying the opportunity for an all-night conversation of the kind they had had frequently when they were younger and Michael and Peggy still in the hills. My own lateness in arriving did not seem out of the ordinary.

They were talking about old times. The warmth of tone of their voices as they spoke indicated that they were remembering things they liked to remember, even though they had often been hard times – times that had meant much to them and so stayed vividly in memory. I focussed my attention automatically. They were talking about work they had done.

Jimmy Paddy talked first, about cutting turf. It was clear that it was something he was good at, and he talked about how many tractor loads he could cut in a season when he was younger, and of the craft of cutting the turf, not swinging your arms and lifting the spade with every cut but flicking your wrist in a quick, agile way so that the turf would fly off the end of the spade up on to the pile of cut pieces on the bank. That way you kept the turf flying, he said, and he remembered proudly the time an old man watching him work had commented that the first piece of turf was still in the air when the next was already flying off the spade.

The others listened attentively and made quiet comments of appreciation and recollection. Then Michael spoke about his days in Scotland, when there was no way to make a living here in Donegal and he had had to leave his farm for a number of years to look for work elsewhere, and had gone to the highlands, where dam building was going on; and how he had had to 'lie out' on the heather at night with only his topcoat for a cover against the rain or even light snow that fell one time until he found work – 'If you would come anywheres near the barracks before you had a job, you would get no job then,' he remembered, 'they would put your name on a list, and there was no job for you then' – so he and the men he was with had stayed away from the barracks and slept out instead, and with the money they had brought along with them they bought potatoes and onions and bacon and had a *drum-up* every night (and here Michael explained for my benefit that a drum-up was an old tin can, with a loop of wire over it as a handle, that he and the others wore at their belts and cooked their supper in over an open fire); and then he had got work; and he talked of life in the barracks living with sixty other men, and of being given the job, with another man, of setting charges of dynamite, and of the good judgement needed in cutting the fuses, so that each fuse would be long enough to allow them to ignite it and the other charges they were laying down at the same time and still have time to get to cover before the detonation; and his mind went to the time his fellow-worker's judgement was slightly off and he cut the fuses too short, and then for some reason lagged behind, and Michael lagged too in order not to leave his mate behind, and they only got through the shower of rocks and debris by a kind of miracle. Michael shook his head wonderingly at the event, and we all commented on the escape, and wondered at it too.

There was a silence and some small talk, and then Peggy told about how she had started working. Her mother had died when she was only thirteen – 'if it was today they would save her,' she said – and as she was the oldest of five she took over the job of looking after the family. A neighbour woman had come in at first to cook and darn clothes for them, but then she had taught Peggy to do those things herself, and Peggy remembered particularly making bread, having to stand on a low stool to be high enough to mix the soda bread in a bowl at the kitchen table – 'for I was too wee, you see' – then getting the mixed dough into the hot iron bastible pot that she had hung while it was still empty over the turf fire, and setting glowing pieces of turf from the fire around the top of the iron pot cover; but she remembered the way she could not get the heavy iron pot off the fire again when the bread was baked, and so had to call her father in – 'in from the fields' – to take it off. 'And so I am baking bread and working since,' she concluded with a broad smile that yet had an element of long weariness in it.

Finally it was Peadar's turn, and his mind went back to his

first hiring-fair, when he was no more than eleven or twelve. He did not talk about the fair itself but about his father taking him by the hand – 'he cotched me by the hand, and away' – and the two of them going over the hills together. What he remembered was the way a heavy mist had come up while they were still in the hills. His father had sat down on a high bank of turf and filled and lit his pipe, and after he had smoked for a while in the mist with the boy sitting beside him he had said: 'I am afraid, Peadar my lad, that we are off the path. I have lost the path.' And what Peadar recalled was his own calmness and optimism, even as a boy, and his face showed his pride, even so many years afterwards, as he told us about how he reassured his father. 'I hope,' he had said, 'I hope the mist will open out.' And what had happened was simple. 'The mist opened out,' Peadar bragged, spreading his arms apart to illustrate the parting of the mist, 'and it made two halves. And my father saw the path.' We smiled. The story indicated that Peadar's mind was on the hill, and I knew he would say more about it later on the way home.

After that the talking flagged, and they all suddenly became aware of the lateness of the hour. Jimmy and Peadar and I got up to go, but Peggy made us sit down again while she made tea – it was what she called 'tea' but it was really breakfast, eggs and bacon and reheated potatoes from yesterday's dinner, and bread and marmalade to go with the hot tea – and so we sat for another hour and idly talked and ate before we finally got started for the hills again. As we walked up the dirt lane towards the road the ice that had formed on the puddles of water in the hollow spots crunched under our feet, and Peadar and Jimmy commented on the frost and the brightness of the stars, and I thought of the road into the hills and of the ice that would have formed on it in the badly drained places. As I started the car and the wheels spun uncertainly at first Peadar chuckled, as he would chuckle when we were on foot at the hardiness of the night and the challenge of the frost, and Jimmy made some comment from the back seat about the slipperiness of the road. The car began its dance and I felt uneasy and increased my concentration, but we went on safely and reached Jimmy's house and I pulled up and let him out. Peadar and I drove on.

The car danced on and I drove more cautiously still,

especially so on the final steep ascent before the road reaches the front door of my own house. The stars gleamed brightly through the bare branches of the thorn trees that stand along the sides of the road there and through the overgrown fuchsia, glittering with that extra intensity that stars seem to have just before the first light of dawn on frosty nights, as though anxious to make the most of the little time that is left to them. Along the right side of the road the water that had run out of the kitchen drain-pipe during the day had frozen into a long ribbon, picked out by the starlight from the surrounding dark ground. I pulled over and stopped on the level ground before the house, then leaned across and pulled the handle to open the door on Peadar's side. We got out. Peadar stood in the middle of the road, about to say good night and start over the shoulder and the hill for his own place, but I urged him to come in for a drink.

He looked about at the sky, as if examining the weather to see if it was going to be dry or wet, as I had seen him do so many times when he was about to make a decision to begin or defer some farm work that needed a dry day, or to wait out a showery period before taking the road after stopping in at some house, or to press on quickly in the interval between showers. It was a gesture of habit, I knew, become involuntary through repetition and time, and that night, with the perfect clearness and dryness of the sky, it stood for the slight hesitation that politeness requires before accepting an invitation.

Then he laughed, really a soft chuckle of pleasure. I knew what he was thinking and what the laugh expressed: that this was like old times, his old times, the long nights he had always enjoyed when he and all his neighbours had been younger and liked sitting up all night, made a regular thing of it, playing cards, dancing, singing, exchanging stories already told many times before, listening attentively as though each retelling were really the first telling, then discussing the story anew and marvelling over it as if never heard before, and so passing the long nights, often until dawn.

'Well,' he said, 'it'd be all right too. I'll just stop in for a moment.' He laughed again. 'There be no hurry on us this hour.'

I opened the door and went in first and Peadar came in and

144

sat down. I lighted the lamp and got out the bottle of whiskey that always sits on the lowest shelf of the food pantry in the far corner of the kitchen, and poured two drinks. We sat and drank and talked, first about the dry cold of the night and the probable coming weather, then about the way we had spent the night, the people we had been with, their lives, their ways, themselves, and so slowly on to the whole life of the hills, each of us seeing it in his own way, I as one who had come into it from the outside, wondering at it even after eleven years, a little in awe, a little puzzled still, Peadar born to it yet feeling something of that awe that I felt, pondering always its mysteries that were so important to him and of which he gave me only glimpses. This night, as on so many, he made an attempt to teach me a little Irish, as if there were something he wanted to explain to me in his own language, as if the learning of that language were a necessary and not very difficult step to the knowledge he had to impart. I felt the compliment behind this thought, and his intention, but my ear and memory were not equal to the opportunity. I garbled the phrases as I tried to repeat them back to him, and after a few repetitions he slowly gave up, as often before.

The attempt had been tied up with some idea, some old event he had been thinking about, and slowly his talk went in that direction, out along the farms and upwards into the hills, remembering long meandering walks across them looking for lost animals, then slowly recollecting things seen and remembered, sudden debilitating hunger and burning thirst, and wild, unusual things not known out of the hills, not seen anywhere but there: the water-horses, the sword-nosed dorhos, the winged eels.

I listened silently while he spoke, but I was tired by then and my attention flagged. Peadar finished his drink. He got up and went to the door and I got up too, my coat still on, to accompany him, as I always had before, the first few hundred yards on his way home. We walked up the shoulder together to the point where the road turned sharply south and down again to the valley and Peadar's path went off into the hill, and stood there, as we had often done, talking about small things we had in common, looking out as we talked over the dim landscape that stretched before us for miles, just visible as it was in the first twilight of early dawn, reluctant to finish our talking and so end this night that seemed to have had something special about it, to have redeemed some moment of an earlier time of life, sensing each other's company the more keenly for being alone, standing together as the world before us still slept.

A little light had crept into the sky to the east but the largest stars were still visible in the blue-black sky, and the waning moon, a thin crescent then, with only a few days of life left before it disappeared to make way for another incarnation of itself, lay on its back near the eastern hills, one bright star centred just above it as though cradled between its horns.

Looking at it, I thought of the passing of the old month, but Peadar's mind went ahead to the coming seasons, the end of winter, the return of spring and with it the resumption of the annual round of work always so welcome to him: the lambing first, then the digging of the ground and sowing the crop of corn and spuds, cutting the turf, mowing the hay, and so on through the year, a kind of spoken synopsis of the yearly repetition of the natural world that he was himself so much a part of and that I was glad to share in, even briefly. And then his mind went to the legends of the hills again, and he began to speak of the three men now living for whose sake the world was still in existence. I determined to listen carefully as he spoke, and thought I did, but my mind was on the crescent moon lying on its back in the east, with the star, almost touching it, just above it. I thought of how the old moon would disappear, to be replaced in a few days by a new crescent in the west at evening, and as Peadar talked, interjecting phrases of Irish between the English ones, as though in explanation of thoughts that could never be expressed in any other tongue, I wondered what the new moon would be like when it came. Then my mind returned to what Peadar was saying, but I realized that he had finished speaking, and that I had not actually listened to what he had told me about the three men, or could not remember it (or had so quickly forgotten), the most mysterious of those legends he was always pondering to himself.

We parted then and I walked back along the road, Peadar over the hill, and as I returned homewards along the road I followed him with my mind as he walked along his path, the one he had made. I thought of him striding over the hill, down into the other valley, through the gate to his lane and across the river and upward again, old now but vigorous still for a while, as the blue dawn grew light above him.

So I carried his image in my mind as I returned home and went to bed, and as I lay there I thought of Peadar pondering the secrets of the earth, and I wondered about them, wondered about the secrets of the earth myself and for the first time perhaps broke through that old barrier of unbelief that I had carried always with me, wore in my thoughts and on my looks when Peadar spoke, a barrier not only to belief but to speech, to Peadar's speech, who was not able, as I saw at last, to speak those inner parts of his knowledge to my unready ears. His mind knew what mine had always refused to know: that words though spoken reach only the willing hearer.

And I wondered, not knowing even then, about Peadar's secrets, the secrets of the earth that he was pondering as he climbed his path along the last long hill on his own homeward walk, and as I wondered and pondered it seemed to me that I too was entering slowly into the secrets, the unspoken thoughts, safe still for a while from profanation, and entering slowly into the earth, slowly, by degrees, and so by stages fell asleep.